EASY AS...123

CREATIVE
CHICKEN

EASY AS...123

CREATIVE
CHICKEN

JENI WRIGHT

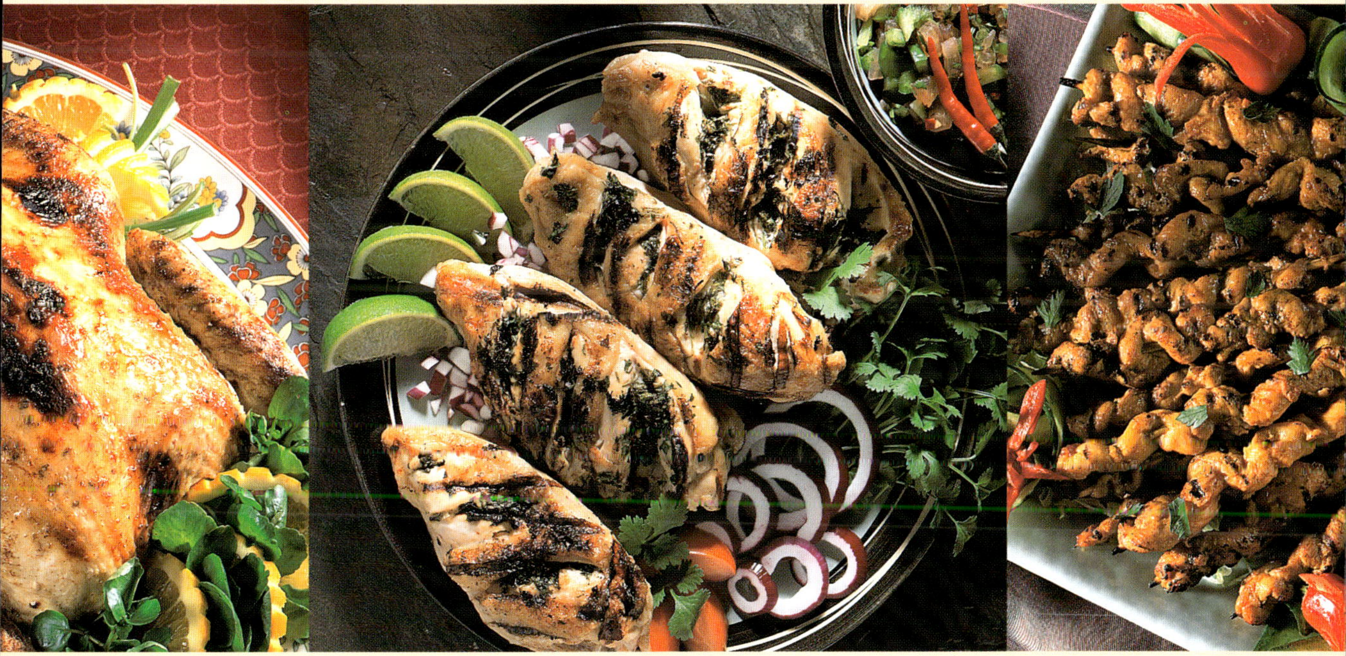

DOUBLEDAY
NEW YORK·LONDON·TORONTO·SYDNEY·AUCKLAND

A CARROLL & BROWN BOOK

Created and produced by
CARROLL & BROWN LIMITED
5 Lonsdale Road
London NW6 6RA

Art Director Chrissie Lloyd
Designer Paul Stradling

Food Stylist Eric Treuillé

Photography David Murray

Production Wendy Rogers

A Main Street Book
Published in the United States by DOUBLEDAY
A division of Bantam Doubleday Dell Publishing Group, Inc.
1540 Broadway
New York
New York 10036

MAIN STREET BOOKS, DOUBLEDAY, and the portrayal of a building with a tree are trademarks of Doubleday, a division of Bantam Doubleday Dell Publishing Group, Inc.

Copyright © 1996 Carroll & Brown Limited
Text Copyright © 1996 Jeni Wright

All rights reserved.

Library of Congress Cataloging-in-Publication Data

Wright, Jeni
  Easy as 1, 2, 3 creative chicken / Jeni Wright. --1st ed.
   p. cm.
  Includes Index
  ISBN 0-385-48203-5
  1. Cookery (Chicken). 2. Quick and easy cookery. I. Title.
  TX750. 5. C45W75 1997
  641.6'65 --dc20   96-5180
               CIP

Reproduced by Colourscan, Singapore

Printed and bound in England by Butler and Tanner Ltd

First American Edition: April 1997

Cover design Chrissie Lloyd
Cover photography David Murray

10 9 8 7 6 5 4 3 2 1

For my children, Oliver and Sophie

CREATIVE CHICKEN

From the sun-ripened flavors of the Mediterranean to the spicy heat of the Orient, chicken lends itself to a great variety of tastes.

In this collection of fifty fabulous recipes there are creative dishes to suit every occasion and every palate – homey roasts and casseroles, quick and easy salads and stir-fries, elegant sautés, and exotic curries. All these recipes are simple to make in just three steps, using fresh, easy-to-find ingredients.

Tips and tricks of the trade are included too, together with clever ideas for garnishes and accompaniments to make these chicken dishes both look and taste really fantastic.

CONTENTS

Basic Techniques 6

Whole Birds 8

Chicken Pieces 28

Boneless Chicken 52

Recipe Index 96

TECHNIQUES

BASIC TECHNIQUES

Trussing, spatchcocking, and quartering are all basic techniques for handling poultry, and apply to a variety of birds, large and small.

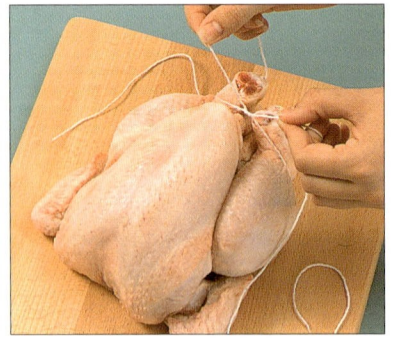 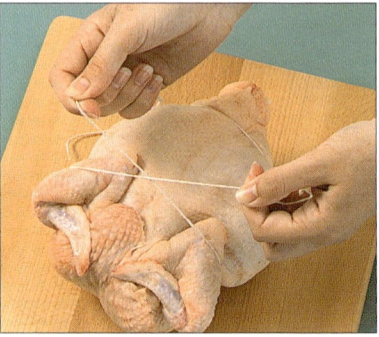 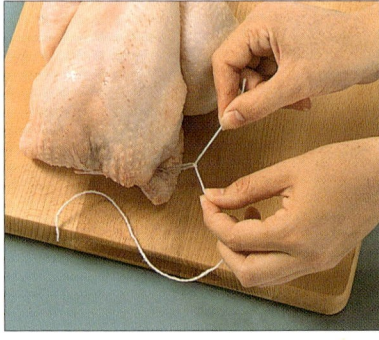

Trussing
Cut a long piece of kitchen string and tie a single knot around the ends of the legs. Pull the string toward the wings, bringing it between the legs and the body.

Turn the bird breast-side-down. Pull the string to cross over the wings, keeping them flat against the bird. Tie the string in a single knot.

Turn the bird breast-side-up, sliding the knot to one side. Tie a double knot to hold the bird in shape, and cut off the excess string.

 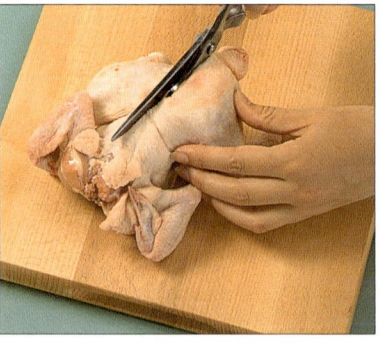 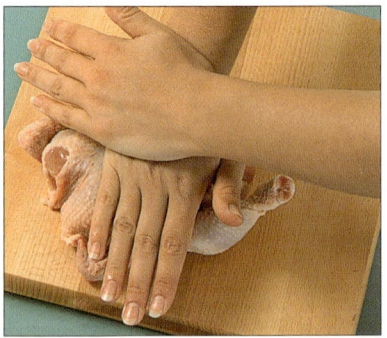

Spatchcocking
With the bird breast-side-up, pull back the skin from the neck and cut around the wishbone with a small knife. Remove the wishbone from the bird. The wishbone can be used for making stock.

Turn the bird over and cut along each side of the backbone with poultry shears. Remove the backbone. The backbone can be used for making stock. Turn the bird breast-side-up.

Push down on the bird to break the breastbone. Keeping the bird flat, push a metal skewer through the wings and breast. Push another skewer through the thighs and bottom end of the breast.

TECHNIQUES

Chicken Stock

A good stock recipe is indispensable. Backbones, necks, wings, and giblets are used to make a hearty base. Roughly chopped vegetables – celery, carrots, and onion are used here, but leeks and mushrooms can be added as well – a big bouquet garni, and a few black peppercorns round out the flavor.

Makes about 1½ qts

Chicken neck, back, and wings
Chicken giblets (except liver)
2 celery stalks, roughly chopped
2 carrots, roughly chopped
1 onion, quartered
1 bouquet garni
5 black peppercorns
Salt

Put all the ingredients in a large pot with 2 qts water. Bring slowly to a boil, skimming the scum as necessary. Simmer, half covered, until well flavored, about 1 hour.

Strain the stock to remove the bones and vegetables. Let cool, then skim the fat from the surface with a slotted spoon. Season the stock with salt just before using.

Quartering
With the bird breast-side-up and using a large knife, cut straight down through the thigh joint to separate each whole leg from the body of the bird.

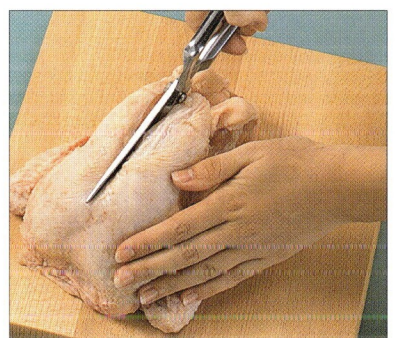

With poultry shears or a large knife, cut the breast in half, cutting straight through the soft breast bone as you go.

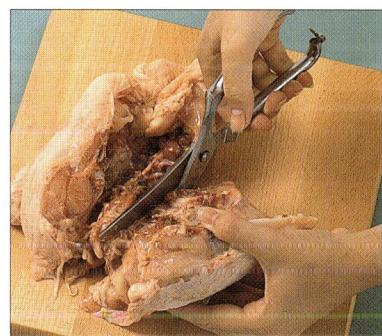

Split open the bird and cut away the breast halves from the backbone, detaching them on both sides. The backbone can be used for making stock.

WHOLE BIRDS

FARMHOUSE CHICKEN IN A POT

Fresh and tangy, with the heady aromas of herbs, cider, and springtime vegetables, this chicken casserole offers a complete taste of the country.

Serves 4

2 tbs canola oil	Salt and freshly ground pepper
3–3½-lb chicken	¾ lb baby carrots
1 tb all-purpose flour	¾ lb baby new potatoes
2 cups dry apple cider	2 leeks, thickly sliced
1 cup chicken stock	¼ cup chopped fresh parsley
1 bouquet garni (see box, right)	

Seasonal choice
Use 1 cup shelled fresh peas or cut green beans instead of the leeks.

BOUQUET GARNI

This is the French term for a bunch of aromatic herbs used for flavoring casseroles, stews, and sauces. You can buy dried bouquets garnis, but fresh ones are the best. To make a classic bouquet garni, use a long piece of string and tie together 6–8 parsley stems, 3–4 thyme sprigs, and 1 bay leaf. For easy removal before serving, tie the string to the pan handle.

1 Heat the oil in a flameproof casserole, add the chicken, and brown on all sides. Lift out and set aside. Sprinkle the flour into the pan and cook, stirring, for 1–2 minutes, then add the cider and stock and bring to a boil.

2 Return the chicken to the pan and add the bouquet garni and salt and pepper to taste. Cover and cook in a preheated 325°F oven for 1¼ hours. Add the vegetables, and baste the chicken with the sauce.

3 Cook for another 30–45 minutes, until the vegetables are tender and the juices of the chicken run clear. Let stand for 10 minutes, then taste the sauce for seasoning and sprinkle with the parsley. Serve hot.

WHOLE BIRDS

Apple-Glazed Cornish Hens

Wonderfully succulent, with a subtle hint of sweetness from the apple juice and honey, these birds make a substantial meal. Serve with simple accompaniments such as steamed new potatoes in their skins and crisp green beans.

Serves 4

1 dessert apple, quartered	Finely grated zest and juice of 1 large lemon
4 1¾–2-lb rock Cornish hens	1 tb balsamic vinegar
¼ cup butter, softened	Apple and lemon slices and flat-leaf parsley sprigs for garnish
Salt and freshly ground pepper	
½ cup apple juice	
2 tbs clear honey	

ROCK CORNISH HENS

*Also called rock Cornish game hens, these tiny chickens are specially bred to be small in size when mature, unlike **poussins**, which are simply baby chickens. Rock Cornish hens are a cross between Cornish chickens and White Rock chickens, hence their name. The flesh is tender and juicy, but their frame is quite large for their body, so a 2-lb hen will serve only one person. They are excellent roasted whole as in this recipe, or they can be spatchcocked (page 6) and grilled. Spatchcocked birds are also good broiled, as in the recipe for Cornish Hens with Shallots and Lemon on page 16.*

1 Place an apple quarter inside each hen, set the hens in a roasting pan, and make cuts in the flesh. Brush with the butter, and sprinkle with salt and pepper. Mix together the remaining ingredients, except the garnish, and pour over the hens.

2 Roast the hens in a preheated 375°F oven for 1¼ hours or until the juices run clear. Turn the hens 3–4 times during roasting, and baste well with the cooking juices. Remove from the pan and let stand, covered with foil, for 10 minutes.

3 Skim off the excess fat from the cooking juices, place the pan on top of the stove, and boil, stirring, until slightly reduced. Arrange the hens on a warmed platter, garnish, and serve at once. Pass the cooking juices separately.

WHOLE BIRDS

CELEBRATION ROAST CHICKEN

A mixed herb stuffing and lemon-flavored gravy transform a regular roast chicken into a very special dish. Serve with traditional vegetables for a celebratory family meal.

Serves 4

2 cups lemon-herb stuffing (see box, right)	2 tbs all-purpose flour
	2 cups hot chicken stock
3½–4-lb chicken	
2 tbs canola oil	2 tbs fresh lemon juice
Salt and freshly ground pepper	

Special touches
For a change, you can use orange zest and juice instead of lemon, and tarragon instead of parsley.

LEMON-HERB STUFFING

This light stuffing is quick and easy to make, and it will keep in the refrigerator for up to 2 days if you want to get ahead. To make the stuffing, put 2 cups fresh white breadcrumbs in a bowl and stir in the finely grated zest of 1 lemon, 2 tbs fresh lemon juice, ⅓ cup chopped fresh parsley, 1 tsp dried thyme or sage, 1 beaten egg, and salt and pepper to taste. If your family likes extra stuffing, make double the quantity, spoon half into a lightly oiled baking dish, and level the surface. Dot the top with butter, and bake in the oven with the chicken for the last 30 minutes of roasting time.

1 Spoon the stuffing into the neck cavity of the chicken, fold over the flap of skin, and secure with the wings. Set the chicken in a roasting pan just big enough to hold it, brush it all over with the oil, and sprinkle with salt and pepper.

2 Roast in a preheated 350°F oven for 1¾ hours or until the juices run clear, basting occasionally and covering with foil if the skin is too brown. Remove from the pan and let stand, covered with foil, for 10 minutes. Pour off all but about 1 tb fat from the pan.

3 Set the pan on top of the stove, add the flour, and stir over moderate heat for 1–2 minutes. Add the stock and lemon juice and stir until thickened. Taste for seasoning. Carve the chicken and serve at once, with the gravy passed separately.

WHOLE BIRDS

ORANGE-SOY CHICKEN

The crisp skin and tender flesh of this whole roasted bird are given an Asian flavor with a sweet and sour mixture of soy sauce, wine vinegar, and honey. Garlic and spices give pungency, and orange juice adds a fresh and fruity flavor.

FIVE-SPICE POWDER

This aromatic mixture of five different finely ground spices is used quite frequently in both Chinese and Vietnamese cooking. It has a wonderfully fragrant smell, and tastes both sweet and mildly peppery. The five spices that make up the powder are star anise, cloves, **cassia** *(a bark similar to cinnamon), fennel seeds, and* **fagara**, *the dried berry of the Chinese ash tree, also known as Sichuan pepper.*

Serves 4

1 orange, quartered	2 tbs wine vinegar
3½–4-lb chicken	2 garlic cloves, minced
1 tsp salt	1–2 cups chicken stock
1 tsp five-spice powder (see box, right)	¼ cup dry sherry
	1 tb clear honey
½ tsp chili powder	Orange slices and salad greens for garnish
1 cup fresh orange juice	
2 tbs soy sauce	

1 Put the orange quarters inside the chicken. Prick the chicken all over, then place on a rack in a roasting pan. Mix the salt and spices and rub over the chicken. Mix together half the orange juice, the soy sauce, vinegar, and garlic. Brush over the chicken.

2 Roast in a preheated 350°F oven for 1¾–2 hours until the juices run clear. Turn the chicken and prick frequently during roasting, each time adding a little stock to prevent the juices from drying out. Remove the chicken and let stand, covered with foil.

3 Spoon off the fat from the pan and set the pan on top of the stove. Add any remaining stock and the orange juice, sherry, and honey and bring to a boil, stirring vigorously. Garnish the chicken and serve at once, with the sauce passed separately.

WHOLE BIRDS

Cornish Hens with Shallots and Lemon

Elegant simplicity – and speed – are the hallmarks of this dish. The hens are simply broiled with olive oil and seasonings, then topped with shallots and lemon juice. The end result is light and piquant.

Serves 4

4 1¾–2-lb rock Cornish hens, spatchcocked (page 6)	¼ cup fresh lemon juice
½ cup virgin olive oil (see box, right)	½ cup finely chopped fresh herbs such as parsley, tarragon, or rosemary (optional)
Salt and freshly ground pepper	
2 shallots, very finely chopped	

Special touches
Use finely chopped garlic or sun-dried tomatoes instead of the shallots.

OLIVE OIL

The different types of olive oil – most of which come from the Mediterranean and California – are confusing. "Extra-virgin" comes from the first cold pressing of the olives and has a very low acidity level. It is the fruitiest and best, and therefore the most expensive. Use it for salad dressings and cold dishes as its flavor will be marred by cooking. "Virgin" olive oil has a higher acidity level than extra-virgin, and is a good olive oil to use in cooking. It may be cold or hot pressed, depending on the brand, so be sure to check the label. Cold pressed is preferable. Other olive oils labeled "superfine," "fine," and "pure" have acidity levels similar to virgin.

1 Prick the birds all over with a metal skewer. With the birds breast-side-up, thread a skewer through both wings of each bird and another through both legs. This will keep the birds flat during broiling.

2 Put the birds skin-side-up on the rack of the broiler pan, brush each one with 1 tb oil, and sprinkle with salt and pepper. Broil 4 inches from the heat for 20 minutes. Turn the birds over, baste with the pan juices, and broil another 10 minutes.

3 Whisk the shallots with the remaining oil, the lemon juice, and the fresh herbs if using. Transfer the birds to a serving dish, pour the shallot mixture over them, and cover tightly with foil. Let stand at room temperature for 10 minutes before serving.

WHOLE BIRDS

FRENCH ROAST CHICKEN

This method of cooking a whole bird results in wonderfully moist and tender flesh and a rich flavorsome sauce. There are three simple secrets – cover the delicate breast flesh in herb and garlic butter, place a lemon inside the body cavity, and baste with wine and stock during roasting.

Serves 4

¼ cup chopped mixed fresh herbs, such as tarragon and flat-leaf parsley	Salt and freshly ground pepper
	½ cup dry white wine
2 garlic cloves, finely chopped	2 cups chicken stock
¼ lb unsalted butter, softened	Fresh herb sprigs and roasted shallots (see box, right) for garnish
3½–4-lb free-range chicken	
1 lemon	

ROASTED SHALLOTS

These are a great favorite with roasted poultry and meats in France. The flesh cooks down to a kind of paste that can be squeezed out of the skin and spread on the meat before eating, or you can spread it on toasted croûtes (page 20) and serve them alongside soups and stews. Any kind of shallots can be used, but "banana" shallots, available at gourmet markets, are a more interesting shape than the usual rounded ones. Put the shallots, in their skins, in a lightly oiled baking dish and drizzle with 1–2 tbs virgin olive oil. Roast them in the oven with the chicken for the last 40 minutes of cooking time.

1 Beat the chopped herbs and garlic into the butter. Ease your fingers between the breast skin and flesh of the bird and spread the butter evenly over the flesh. Prick the lemon all over with a fork and place inside the bird.

2 Put the chicken on a rack in a roasting pan, sprinkle with salt and pepper, and pour the wine and 1 cup stock over it. Roast in a preheated 375°F oven for 1½ hours or until the juices run clear, basting frequently and adding more stock if the pan becomes dry.

3 Remove the chicken from the pan and let stand, covered with foil, for 10 minutes. Spoon off the fat from the pan, add the remaining stock, and boil, stirring, until slightly reduced. Garnish the chicken and serve hot, with the juices passed separately.

WHOLE BIRDS

CHICKEN WITH FORTY GARLIC CLOVES

This famous recipe comes from Provence in the south of France, where purple-skinned garlic grows in abundance. Be sure to do what the French do – lift the cover of the casserole at the table so that the aroma of the garlic can be fully appreciated.

CROUTES

Although a large number of garlic cloves is used in this recipe, you will be amazed how mellow and sweet they taste. The best way to enjoy roasted garlic is to squeeze the soft flesh out of the skins and spread it on croûtes. To make toasted croûtes, cut a French baguette diagonally into slices about ½-inch thick and broil the slices on both sides until they are crisp and golden. To keep the croûtes warm until serving time, wrap them in a clean dish towel.

Serves 4

3½–4-lb chicken	40 garlic cloves, unpeeled
Salt and freshly ground pepper	¼ cup all-purpose flour
1 large bouquet garni (page 8)	Toasted croûtes (see box, right) for serving
¼ cup virgin olive oil	

Finishing touches
If you like, pour ¼ cup cognac over the bird just before serving.

1 Season the chicken inside and out, put the bouquet garni inside, and truss (page 6) to keep a tidy shape. Heat the oil in a flameproof casserole and brown the chicken on all sides. Lift the chicken out.

2 Place the garlic cloves in the casserole, set the chicken on top, and cover with a tight-fitting lid. Mix the flour to a paste with about 1 tb water and spread around the edge of the lid to seal.

3 Bake the chicken and garlic in a preheated 375°F oven for 1¾ hours without opening the oven door. Serve hot, straight from the casserole, with toasted croûtes alongside.

WHOLE BIRDS

BABY CHICKENS WITH PANCETTA

Crisply roasted pancetta and creamy mascarpone give these little birds an Italian flavor, and at the same time keep the breast flesh moist and tender. Serve one bird per person for an informal Sunday lunch.

Serves 4

4 1-lb baby chickens (see box, right)	2 tbs chopped fresh marjoram or oregano
Salt and freshly ground pepper	
4 garlic cloves, peeled and halved	12 slices pancetta
¾ cup mascarpone cheese	

Special touches
If you like, use crème fraîche instead of the mascarpone, and bacon instead of the pancetta.

BABY CHICKENS

*These little birds, known as **poussins** or **petits poussins** in French, are from 4 to 6 weeks old and weigh no more than 1¼ lbs, which is just enough for one serving. Their flesh is young and therefore tender, but they tend to lack the flavor of more mature birds. The best baby chickens to buy are free range because these have more flavor – look for them in large supermarkets and gourmet stores. Roasting is the best cooking method for poussins, but to maintain tenderness, you should protect the delicate breast flesh. You can also marinate the birds before cooking, and put a moist stuffing in the neck end.*

1 Season the inside of the birds with salt and pepper, then place 2 pieces of garlic inside each one. Lift up the breast skin and spread 1 tb mascarpone over each breast. Sprinkle each breast with 1 tsp chopped herbs and pepper to taste.

2 Place the birds in a roasting pan and wrap 3 pancetta slices around each bird. Roast in a preheated 400°F oven for 1 hour or until the juices run clear when the flesh is pierced in the thickest part. Remove the birds from the pan.

3 Set the pan on top of the stove and stir the remaining mascarpone into the juices. Simmer, stirring, for 1–2 minutes until golden brown. Serve the chickens sprinkled with the remaining herbs, with the sauce passed separately.

WHOLE BIRDS

JERKED CHICKEN

Jerked meat is one of Jamaica's most famous specialties. Here jerk paste is spread on a chicken, which is grilled over charcoal. Hot and spicy from chilies and peppercorns and pungent with allspice and cinnamon, the flavor of the crust permeates the bird.

Serves 4

2 small onions	1 dried red chili, halved
3 whole cloves	2 tsps ground allspice
2 garlic cloves, peeled and halved	½ tsp ground cinnamon
2 tbs canola oil	1 tsp salt
2 tsps black peppercorns, crushed	3½–4-lb chicken

Special touches
Place a few fresh thyme sprigs on the barbecue grill under the chicken.

GRILLING WHOLE BIRDS

A kettle-style barbecue makes grilling a whole bird really easy – all you have to do is put the bird on the grill and cover with the lid. The bird will cook by itself without needing to be basted or turned, the skin will become beautifully crisp and dark, and the flesh will be moist and meltingly tender. Some kettle barbecues have a special holder for whole birds and roasts, but this is not essential. Simply put both grills on the barbecue with the drip pan between them, then place the bird on the top grill. If you have only one grill, stand the bird on a rack in a roasting pan and then place the pan on the grill.

1 Stud 1 onion with the cloves and put inside the chicken. Chop the remaining onion and put in a food processor with the garlic, oil, peppercorns, chili, ground spices, and salt. Work to a paste.

2 Slash the skin of the bird quite deeply with a sharp knife and spread the jerk paste all over, working it into the cuts. Cover and marinate in the refrigerator for at least 2 hours, preferably overnight.

3 Put the chicken, breast-side-up, on the barbecue grill (see box, above). Cover and cook for 1½ hours or until the juices run clear when the thickest part of a thigh is pierced. Serve hot or cold.

WHOLE BIRDS

CHICKEN SOUP CREOLE

Here a whole bird is simmered in a flavorful tomato-based stock, then the meat is removed from the bones and combined with rice and okra to make a deliciously spicy main course soup.

Serves 4

2–2½-lb chicken	A few drops hot pepper sauce, or more to taste
½ lb ripe tomatoes, roughly chopped	Salt and freshly ground pepper
1 onion, roughly chopped	½ cup long-grain rice
2 celery stalks, roughly chopped	½ lb young fresh okra (see box, right), sliced
1 chicken bouillon cube, crumbled	Fresh thyme sprigs for garnish
2 tbs tomato paste	
A few sprigs fresh thyme	

OKRA

This long, tapering, five-sided vegetable – known in England as ladies fingers, and in India as **bhindi** *– is at its best when young and fresh. The season for young, tender okra is from May to October, when you should look for bright green pods that are no more than 4 inches long. Choose firm okra that snap cleanly rather than bend, and avoid any that are limp and brown at the tip or around the edges. The juice of the okra is valued in Creole cooking as a thickening agent, and the soups and stews of New Orleans, the most famous of which has to be gumbo, often include okra among their ingredients for this very reason.*

1 Put the chicken in a large pan with all the ingredients except the rice and okra. Add 6 cups water and bring to a boil. Cover and poach gently for 1½ hours or until the chicken is tender. Let the chicken cool in the stock, then lift it out onto a cutting board.

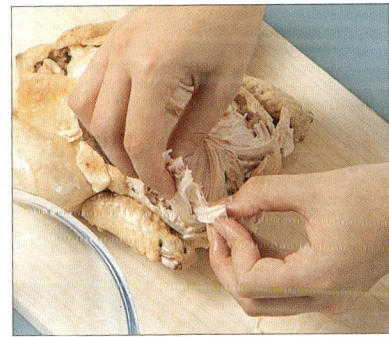

2 Remove the meat from the carcass and shred it into bite-sized pieces. Discard the skin. Strain the stock and chill for about 4 hours, then remove any fat from the surface. Bring the stock to a boil in a clean pan, add the rice, and simmer for 10 minutes.

3 Add the okra and simmer for another 10 minutes until tender. Add the chicken and heat through, then taste for seasoning and add more hot pepper sauce if you like. Serve hot, in warmed bowls, garnished with fresh thyme sprigs.

CHICKEN PIECES

SHAKER CHICKEN

With its rich creamy sauce and sweet apple slices, this chicken casserole makes the perfect family dinner. Serve it in simple Shaker style with bowls of steaming mashed potatoes and crisply cooked fresh vegetables.

Serves 4

8 skinless free-range chicken thighs	2–2½ cups hot chicken stock
Salt and freshly ground pepper	2 bay leaves, torn
¼ cup butter	⅓ cup heavy cream
4 Red Delicious apples	Red Delicious apple slices and fresh bay leaves for garnish
1 tb dark brown sugar	
½ tsp ground allspice or cinnamon	

SHAKER COOKING

The Shakers, who were at their height in New England and the Midwest in the nineteenth century, believed in eating and living simply. Renowned for their self-sufficiency, they lived off the land and grew all their own food. They had their own livestock, dairies, orchards, herb, and vegetable gardens. Although some followed a strict vegetarian diet, the majority enjoyed plenty of meat and poultry dishes, and these were often enriched with home-produced butter, cream, and eggs. This chicken casserole is typically Shaker in that it combines chicken with apples, cream, and herbs, with a subtle touch of spiciness.

1 Season the chicken thighs with salt and pepper. Melt the butter in a large saucepan, add the chicken, and sauté until browned on all sides. Remove from the heat, lift out the chicken with a slotted spoon, and set aside.

2 Quarter and peel the apples, then core and slice them. Return the casserole to the heat and add the apples, sugar, spice, 2 cups stock, and the bay leaves. Simmer for 15 minutes, stirring the apples frequently.

3 Return the chicken to the pan, cover, and simmer for 30 minutes or until tender, adding more stock if necessary. Add the cream and heat through, then taste the sauce for seasoning. Serve hot, garnished with apple slices and bay leaves.

CHICKEN PIECES

GRILLED CHICKEN WITH HOT CHILI SALSA

Serve this spicy Mexican-style chicken sizzling hot, with a chilled bell pepper-and-tomato salsa alongside. The contrast in temperatures is sensational.

Serves 4

4 large chicken breast halves, on the bone	1 green bell pepper, cored, seeded, and chopped
⅓ cup virgin olive oil	1 small hot red chili (see box, right), cored, seeded, and chopped
Juice of 2 limes	
⅓ cup chopped fresh coriander (cilantro)	Salt and freshly ground pepper
2 large garlic cloves, finely chopped	4 lime wedges for serving
4 ripe tomatoes, peeled, seeded, and chopped	

RED HOT CHILIES

*One of the hottest red chilies is the Mexican **pico de pajoro** or "bird's beak" chili. A relation of the more commonly known **arbol** chili, which it closely resembles in shape, it is a favorite ingredient in Mexican salsa and pickles, especially **escabeches**. You can find these chilies both fresh and dried at gourmet markets – either is suitable for this salsa.*

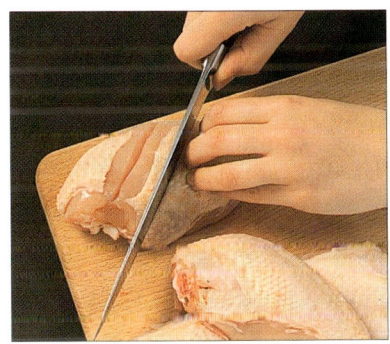

1 Score the chicken breasts with a sharp knife and place in a non-metallic dish. Mix together half the oil and lime juice, and half the coriander and garlic. Pour over the chicken, cover, and marinate at room temperature for 1 hour.

2 Meanwhile, make the salsa. Combine the remaining oil, lime juice, coriander, and garlic in a bowl with the tomatoes, bell pepper, and chili. Mix well, and add salt and pepper to taste. Cover and chill until serving time.

3 Grill the chicken breasts for 5–8 minutes on each side until tender, brushing occasionally with the marinade from the dish. Serve hot, with lime wedges for squeezing. Pass the bowl of salsa separately.

CHICKEN PIECES

Tarragon Cream Chicken

A traditional French recipe is given a new twist with exotic chanterelles. Rich and creamy, it makes an impressive dinner party main course. The added bonus is that it can be made in less than an hour.

TARRAGON

There are two types of tarragon – French and Russian. French tarragon has the delicate flavor of anise, while Russian tarragon is strong and often bitter. Tarragon and chicken have a natural affinity and are frequently teamed in classic French cooking, especially with butter and cream. Always add tarragon at the end of cooking because its subtle flavor is quick to disperse.

Serves 4

2 tbs butter	Salt and freshly ground pepper
1 tb canola oil	1 cup chicken stock
4 chicken breast halves, on the bone	½ cup dry white wine
½ lb wild mushrooms, such as chanterelles, sliced	1 cup crème fraîche
	2 tbs chopped fresh tarragon
1 tsp herbes de Provence	Fresh tarragon sprigs for garnish
2 garlic cloves, finely chopped	

1 Melt the butter with the oil in a flameproof casserole, add the chicken, and brown on all sides. Cover with the mushrooms, and sprinkle with the dried herbs, garlic, and salt and pepper to taste.

2 Add the stock and wine and bring to a boil. Cover and simmer gently for 25 minutes or until the chicken is tender. Lift out the chicken and mushrooms and set aside, then boil the sauce until reduced by about half.

3 Add the crème fraîche and chopped tarragon and stir until thickened. Taste for seasoning. Serve the chicken sliced off the bone, coated with the mushrooms and sauce, and garnished with tarragon sprigs.

CHICKEN PIECES

Chicken with Red Wine and Grapes

A modern version of the classic French *coq au vin*, this chicken casserole is light and fruity. The only accompaniments needed are a bowl of mixed crisp salad leaves and a bottle of fruity red wine.

Serves 4

2 tbs virgin olive oil	Salt and freshly ground pepper
1 red onion, thinly sliced	1 cup fruity red wine, such as Beaujolais
1 garlic clove, finely chopped	1 cup chicken stock
¼ cup sun-dried tomatoes in olive oil (see box, right), thinly sliced	½ lb seedless red or black grapes, halved
4 chicken breast halves, on the bone	1 tsp sugar
1 tb all-purpose flour	

> **SUN-DRIED TOMATOES**
>
> *These are exactly what their name suggests – ripe fresh tomatoes that have been allowed to dry naturally in the hot sun, which is why their flavor is so intense and sweet. The kind that are packed in olive oil are the most convenient because they can be used just as they are, whereas those in cellophane packages need to be soaked in oil or hot water to make them soft enough to slice before use. A jar of sun-dried tomatoes makes a great pantry item – they're indispensable for adding a rich flavor and color to so many cooked dishes, salads, sauces, dressings, and even sandwich fillings.*

1 Heat the oil in a large pan, add the onion, garlic, and sun-dried tomatoes, and cook gently for 5 minutes or until softened. Add the chicken, sprinkle with the flour and salt and pepper to taste, and sauté for 5 minutes until browned.

2 Pour in the wine and let it sizzle, then add the stock and bring to a boil. Cover and simmer for 20 minutes or until the chicken feels tender when pierced with a fork. Remove the chicken from the pan and set it aside.

3 Boil the sauce until reduced slightly, add the grapes and sugar, and simmer gently for 5 minutes. Taste for seasoning. Cut each breast crosswise in half through the bone, return to the pan, and gently heat through. Serve hot.

Marinated Grilled Chicken

Chicken is a superb meat to cook on the barbecue. When steeped in a flavorsome marinade overnight and grilled next day, it becomes charred and crispy on the outside, with succulent and juicy meat underneath.

Tandoori Chicken

Serves 4

4 chicken quarters

1 cup plain yogurt

2 tbs lime juice

1-inch piece fresh ginger root, peeled and crushed

1 garlic clove, minced

¼ cup chopped fresh coriander

1 tb garam masala or curry powder

1 tsp salt

½ tsp chili powder

A few drops red food coloring (optional)

1 Place the chicken pieces in a shallow non-metallic dish and score the flesh deeply with a sharp knife.

2 Mix the remaining ingredients and pour over the chicken. Cover and marinate in the refrigerator overnight.

3 Grill the chicken for 20–25 minutes, turning frequently and brushing with the marinade from the dish, until the juices run clear. Serve hot or cold.

Honey-Mustard Chicken

Serves 4

12 chicken thighs

2 tbs clear honey

2 tbs Dijon-style mustard

1 tb virgin olive oil

1 tb fresh lemon juice

1 garlic clove, finely chopped

Freshly ground pepper

Lemon wedges for serving

1 Place the chicken thighs, skin-side-up, in a shallow non-metallic dish and score the flesh deeply with a sharp knife.

2 Mix together the next 5 ingredients, brush over the chicken, and sprinkle liberally with pepper. Cover and marinate in the refrigerator overnight.

3 Grill the chicken for 15–20 minutes, turning frequently, until the juices run clear. Serve the chicken hot or cold, with lemon wedges for squeezing.

Deviled Drumsticks

Serves 4

12 chicken drumsticks

3 tbs tomato ketchup

2 tbs coarse-grained mustard

2 tbs wine vinegar

2 tbs soft brown sugar

A few drops Tabasco sauce

½ tsp salt

Canola oil for basting

1 cup chicken stock

1 Place the chicken drumsticks in a shallow non-metallic dish and score the flesh deeply with a sharp knife. Mix together the remaining ingredients except the oil and stock, and brush over the chicken. Cover and marinate in the refrigerator overnight.

2 Remove the drumsticks from the marinade. Grill for 15–20 minutes, turning and basting frequently, until the juices run clear.

3 Put the marinade and stock in a pan and boil, stirring, until thickened. Serve the drumsticks hot or cold, with the sauce for dipping.

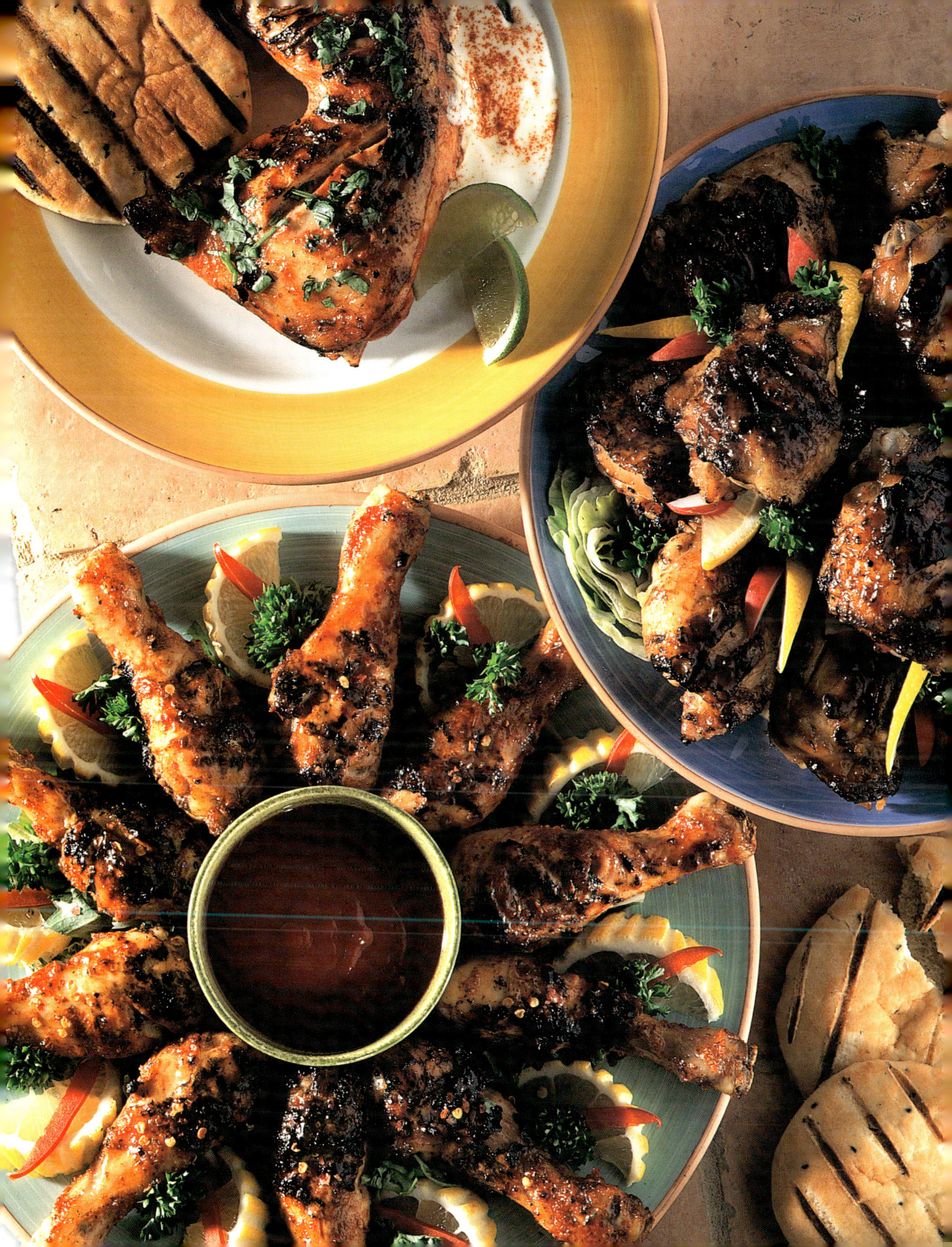

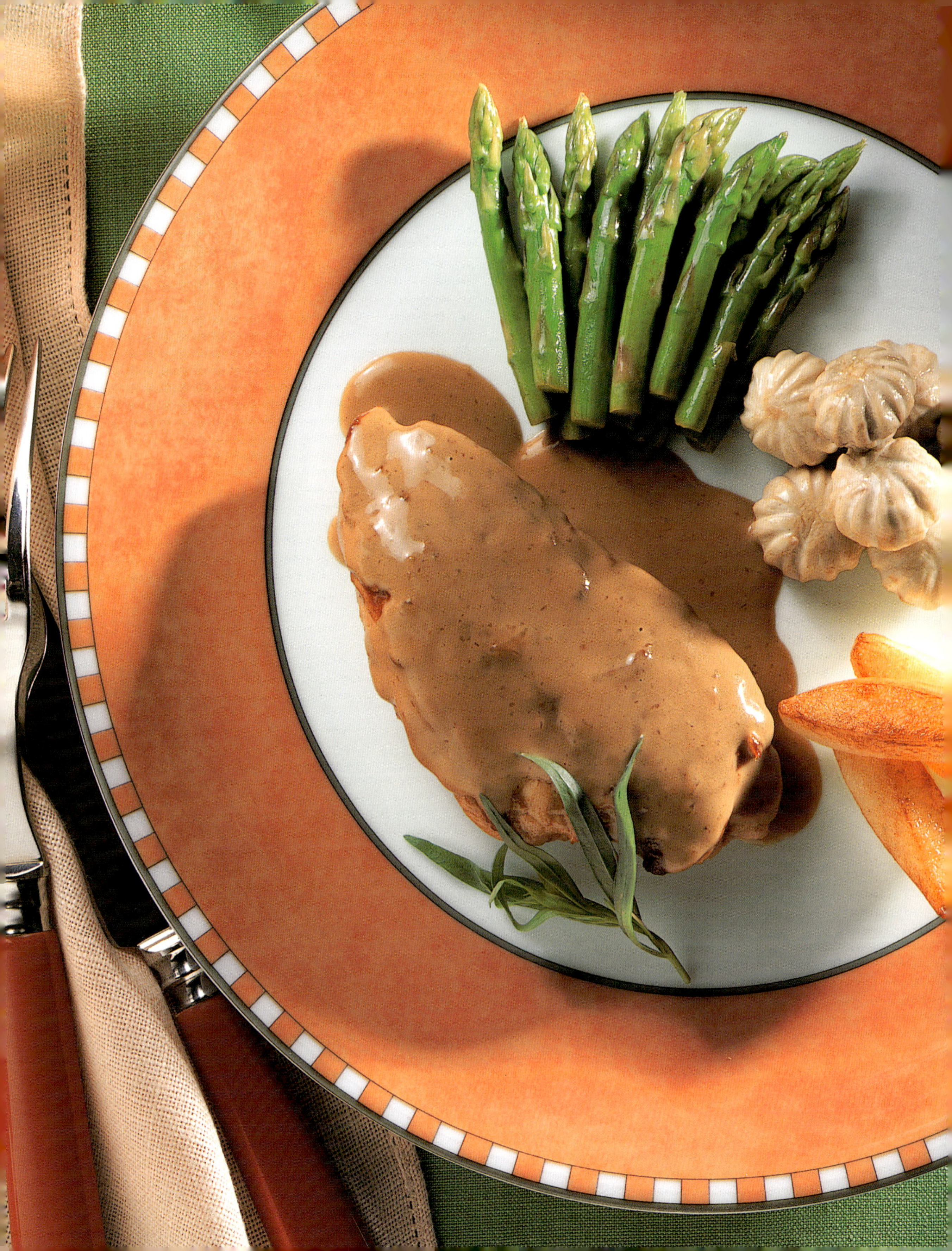

CHICKEN PIECES

ANDALUSIAN CHICKEN

Sherry and garlic are two favorite ingredients of Spanish cuisine, and here they're combined in a truly delicious sauce. Don't be deterred by the number of garlic cloves used – when cooked whole in their skins, their flavor is surprisingly sweet.

ANDALUSIAN COOKING

*This southernmost region of Spain is famous for its sherry, produced around the town of Jerez, from which the drink takes its name. There are numerous different types of sherry, ranging from very light and dry **fino**, through nutty-flavored **amontillado**, to sweet **oloroso**. In the cooking of savory dishes, **amontillado** is the most suitable. Apart from its sherry, which is the most popular aperitif of the region, Andalusia is also well known for its oranges, its sweet desserts, often based on egg yolks, and its tapas. The local gazpacho is unusual in that it is smooth and white, and heavily laced with garlic.*

Serves 6

¼ cup butter	2 tbs sherry vinegar
1 tb virgin olive oil	Salt and freshly ground pepper
6 skinless chicken breast halves, on the bone	½ cup heavy cream
1 head garlic, broken into cloves	Fresh tarragon leaves for garnish
1½ cups medium-dry sherry (see box, right)	

1 Melt the butter with the oil in a flameproof casserole, add the chicken and garlic, and sauté over moderate heat for 10 minutes. Add the sherry and vinegar, and salt and pepper to taste. Cover and simmer gently for 20 minutes or until the chicken is tender.

2 Transfer the chicken to a plate. Strain the cooking liquid, pressing the garlic flesh through the strainer. Return the liquid to the pan, add the cream, and bring to a boil, stirring. Boil for 5 minutes or until the sauce is reduced to a coating consistency.

3 Return the chicken to the pan with the juices that have collected on the plate. Heat through for a few minutes, spooning the sauce over the chicken until it is evenly coated. Taste for seasoning. Serve hot, garnished with tarragon leaves.

CHICKEN PIECES

CHICKEN PAPRIKASH

Richly red and exquisitely sweet, this chicken casserole from Hungary is quick to prepare and cook. Although the flavor is superb when the dish is freshly cooked, it improves if left overnight and reheated the next day.

Serves 4

2 tbs virgin olive oil	1 tb red wine vinegar
2 small red onions, cut lengthwise into wedges	1 tb tomato paste
	1 tsp sugar
1 garlic clove, minced	Salt and freshly ground pepper
1 tb sweet paprika (see box, right)	½ lb cherry tomatoes
¼ tsp caraway seeds	Sour cream for serving
8 skinless chicken thighs	
1 cup chicken stock	

PAPRIKA

Hungarian paprika is not essential for this dish, but it will lend a more authentic taste. The best type to use is sweet paprika, sometimes labeled **süss**, *not the sharp, hot variety, which would make the sauce too pungent for the delicate flavor of the chicken. In Hungary, paprika is often used to spice slowly braised meat stews and casseroles, and the long cooking time mellows the pungency of the sharp spice.*

1 Heat the oil in a flameproof casserole, add the onion, garlic, paprika, and caraway seeds, and cook gently for about 5 minutes. Add the chicken thighs and sauté for about 5 minutes until colored on all sides.

2 Mix together the stock, vinegar, tomato paste, and sugar. Pour over the chicken and bring to a boil. Add salt and pepper to taste, cover, and simmer gently for 25 minutes or until the chicken is just tender.

3 Add the cherry tomatoes and shake the pan vigorously to mix them into the sauce. Cover and simmer for another 5 minutes. Taste for seasoning. Serve hot, with sour cream spooned in the center.

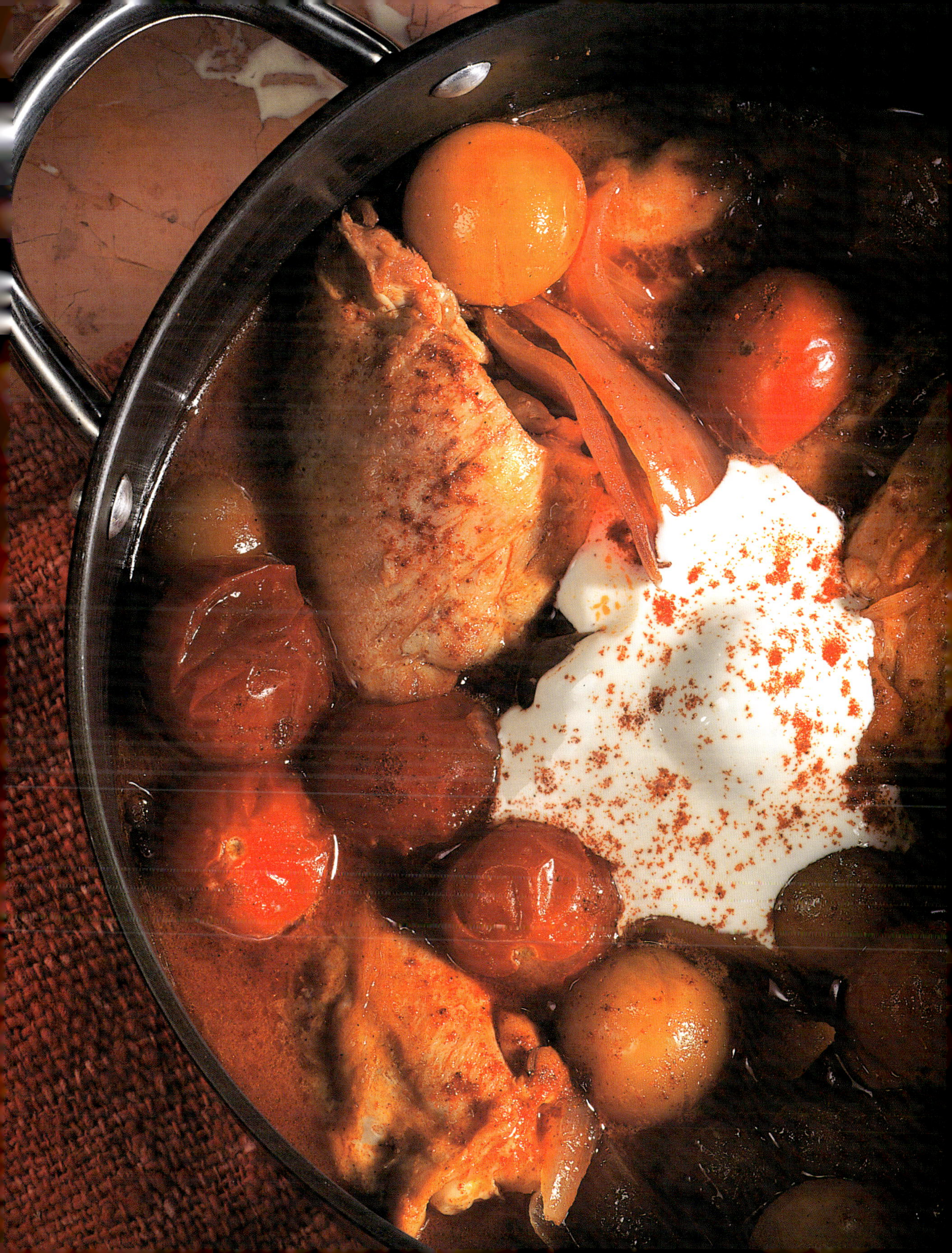

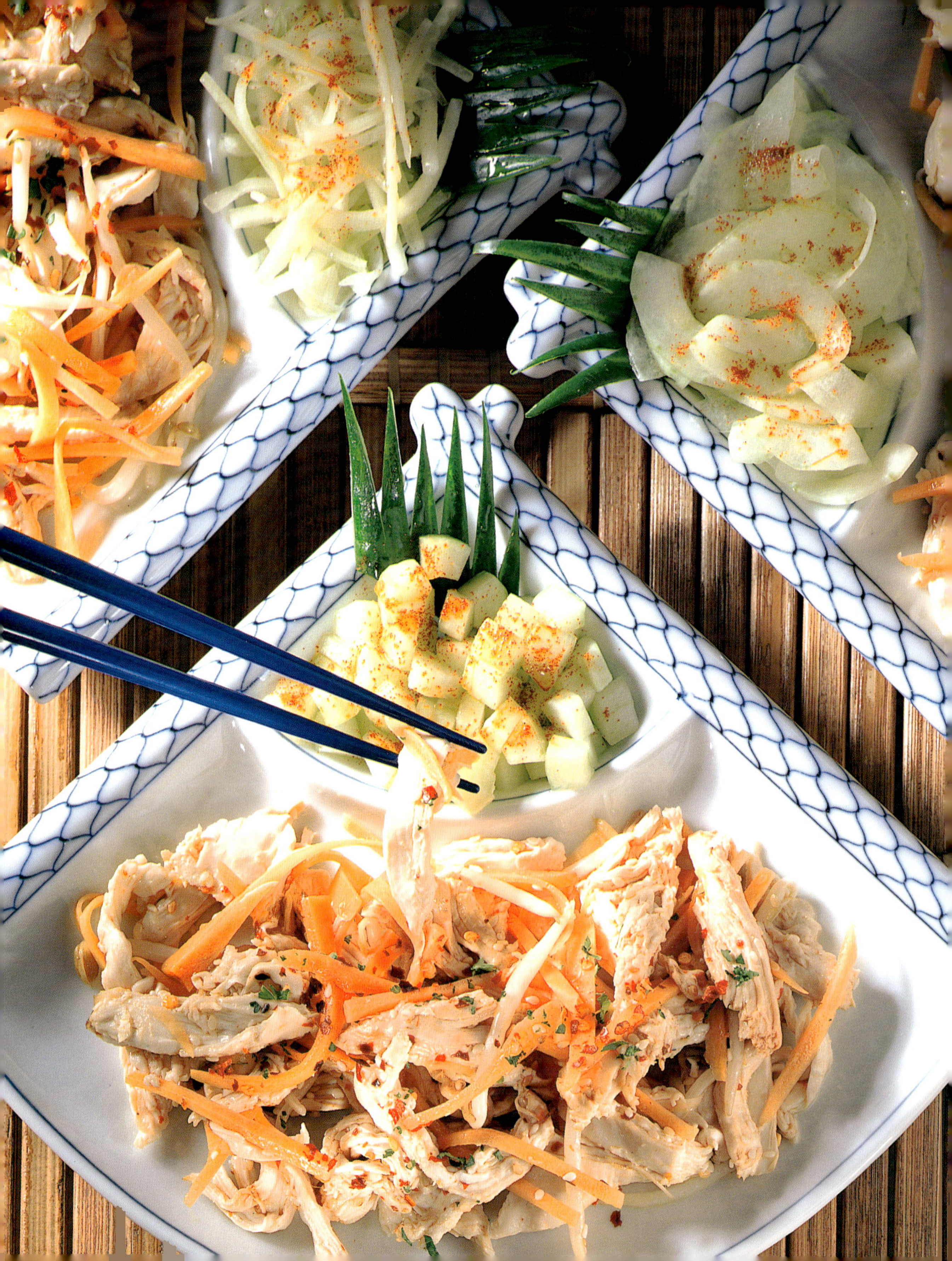

CHICKEN PIECES

Bang Bang Chicken

This curiously named Chinese salad takes its name from the fact that the chicken is pounded – or banged – after cooking. This serves the dual purpose of quickly stripping the flesh from the bones and tenderizing it at the same time.

Serves 4

4 chicken breast halves, on the bone	2 tbs sesame seeds
2 tbs soy sauce	1 tsp crushed dried chilies
1-inch piece fresh ginger root, peeled and sliced	4 carrots, cut into julienne (see box, right)
2 garlic cloves, roughly chopped	1 cup bean sprouts
2 scallions, roughly chopped	2 tbs dry sherry
2 tbs canola oil	1 tsp sugar
1 tb sesame oil	

CARROT JULIENNE

This French term describes food that is cut into fine matchstick strips. In classic French cuisine, vegetables are cut into julienne and used raw as a garnish, while in Chinese cooking they are cut even finer for quick cooking in stir-fries. To julienne a carrot, square off the rounded sides, then cut the carrot into thin slices lengthwise. Stack the slices, then cut lengthwise into strips.

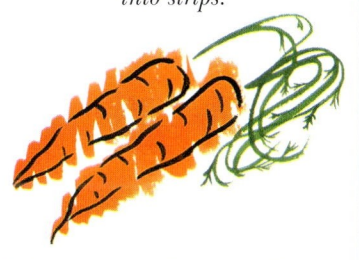

1 Put the chicken in a pan with the soy sauce, ginger, garlic, and scallions. Pour in enough water to cover and bring to a boil. Cover and poach for 20 minutes or until the chicken is just tender. Let cool in the cooking liquid.

2 Remove the chicken from the liquid and pound with a rolling pin to loosen the meat from the bones. Discard the skin, and cut the meat into strips. Heat the oils in a wok, add the sesame seeds and chilies, and stir-fry for about 2 minutes. Remove from the heat.

3 Add the chicken to the wok with the carrots and bean sprouts, and toss to mix. Add ¼ cup of the cooking liquid, the dry sherry, and sugar. Toss again to coat evenly. Marinate at room temperature for 30 minutes before serving.

CHICKEN PIECES

Peppery Chicken

This colorful chicken casserole comes from Sicily, where locally grown bell peppers and chili peppers are frequently used in cooking. The chili is unexpected in an Italian dish, but it gives a welcome piquancy to the overall flavor.

Serves 4

2 tbs virgin olive oil	½ cup dry white wine
4 chicken quarters	3 bell peppers, roasted and cut into thin strips (see box, right)
1 onion, thinly sliced	
2 garlic cloves, finely chopped	Salt and freshly ground pepper
1 small hot red chili, cored, seeded, and chopped	Shredded fresh basil for garnish
14-oz can crushed tomatoes	

ROASTED BELL PEPPERS

Fresh bell peppers (or roasted bell peppers from a jar) can be used in this casserole if you are short of time, but freshly roasted peppers are best. They have a wonderful smoky flavor that goes especially well with the chicken, tomatoes, and white wine. To roast fresh bell peppers, grill or broil them whole until their skins are charred black on all sides, then place them immediately in a plastic bag. Seal the bag and leave until the peppers are cold, then rinse the peppers thoroughly under cold running water and rub off the skins. Pat the flesh dry, and cut lengthwise into very thin slices, discarding the cores and seeds.

1 Heat the oil in a flameproof casserole and brown the chicken on all sides. Remove and set aside. Add the onion, garlic, and chili, and cook gently for about 5 minutes until softened.

2 Add the tomatoes and wine and bring to a boil, stirring. Return the chicken to the casserole, and add the roasted bell pepper strips and salt and pepper to taste.

3 Cover and simmer gently for 30–40 minutes until the chicken is tender. Taste for seasoning. Serve hot, sprinkled with shredded basil.

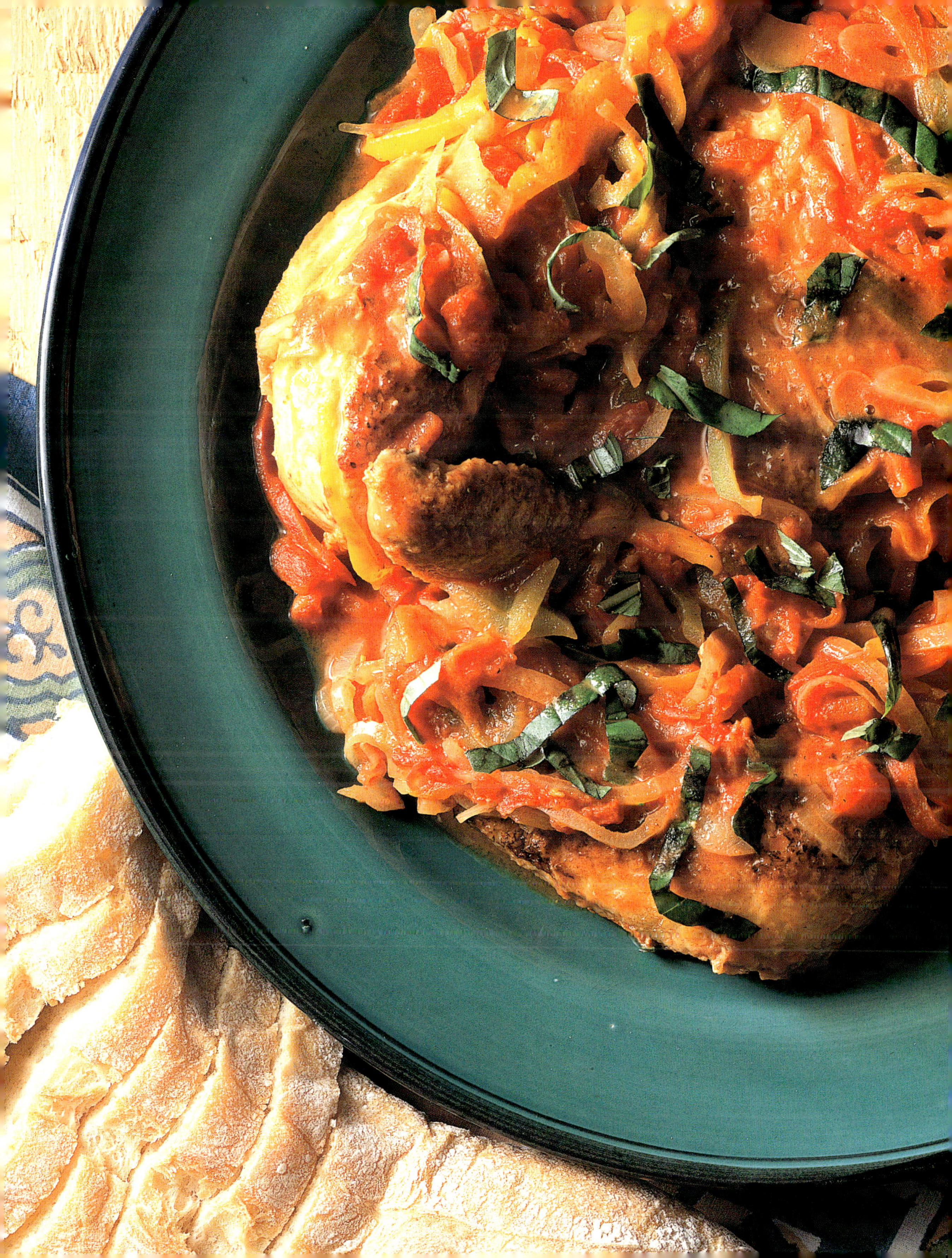

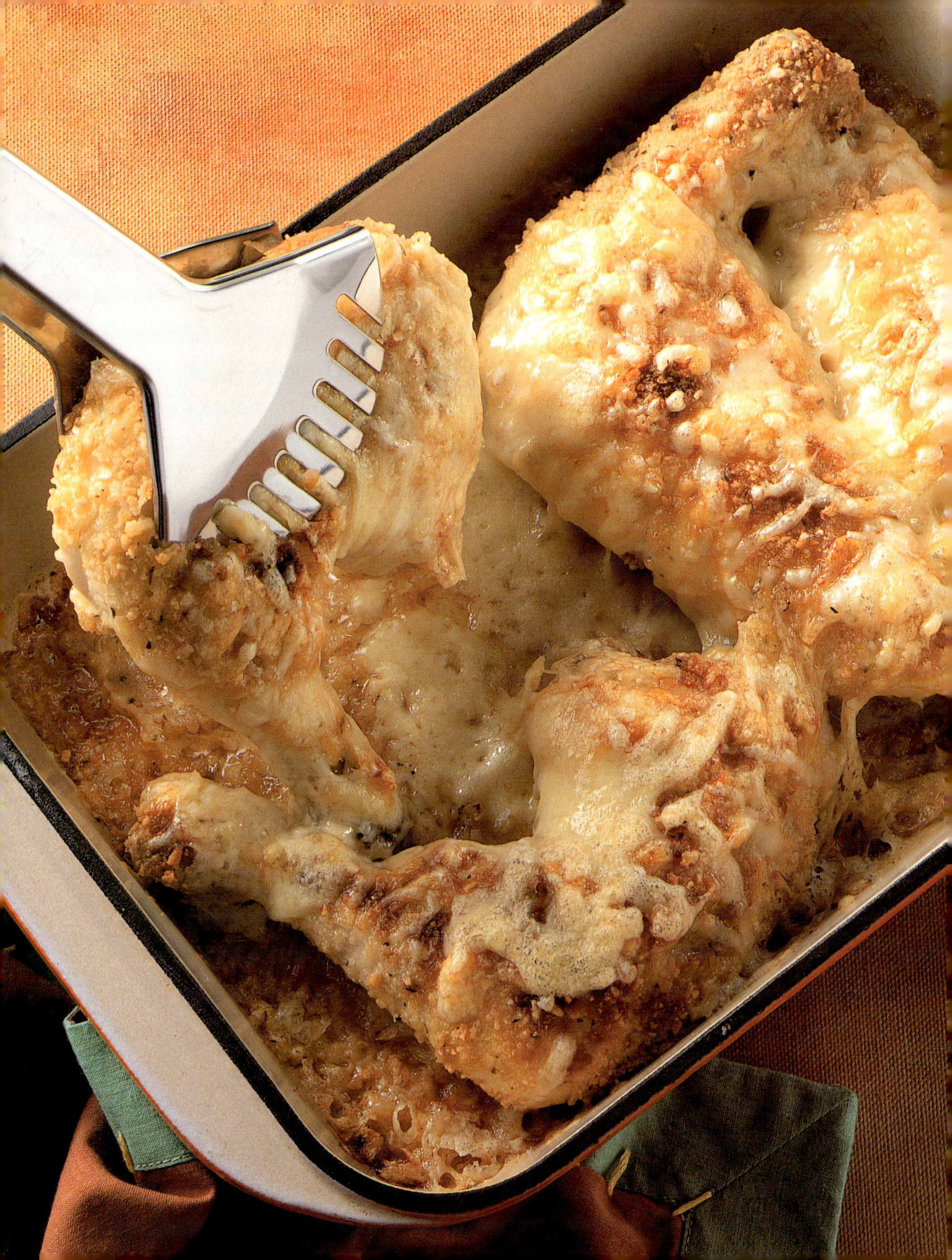

CRISPY CHICKEN

Here, chicken pieces are coated with Parmesan and breadcrumbs, then sprinkled with grated Cheddar, and baked until crisp. The finished dish is crunchy, deliciously rich, and equally good served hot or cold.

Serves 4

1 large egg	½ cup grated Parmesan cheese
1 tsp dry mustard	1 tsp herbes de Provence
Salt and freshly ground pepper	¼ cup butter
4 skinless chicken quarters	¾ cup grated Cheddar cheese
1½ tbs all-purpose flour	
6 tbs dried breadcrumbs (see box, right)	

Special touches
For a picnic, cut each piece of chicken in half so it is easy to eat with the fingers.

> ### DRIED BREADCRUMBS
> *You can use commercially prepared dried breadcrumbs, but they often have coloring added and lack good flavor and texture. Homemade breadcrumbs are quick and easy to make, and a good way of using up stale bread. Cut thin slices of stale bread, remove the crusts, and place the bread in a single layer on a baking tray. Bake in a preheated 300°F oven for about 30 minutes until very dry and golden. Transfer to a food processor and work with the metal blade until very finely ground. Store dried breadcrumbs in an airtight container for up to 1 week, or in the freezer for up to 3 months.*

1 Beat the egg in a dish with the mustard and salt and pepper to taste. Coat the chicken in the flour, then in the egg. Mix together the breadcrumbs, Parmesan, and herbs, and press onto the chicken. Chill, uncovered, for at least 1 hour.

2 Melt the butter and use a little to brush the inside of an ovenproof dish. Arrange the chicken in the dish, sprinkle with the grated Cheddar, and drizzle with the remaining butter.

3 Bake the chicken in a preheated 350°F oven for 40 minutes or until the crust is crisp and golden brown and the flesh feels tender when pierced. Serve hot or cold.

CHICKEN PIECES

SPANISH CHICKEN AND RICE

A quick and easy version of *paella*, this dish uses the tasty combination of chicken, mussels, and chorizo sausage. Serve it with jugs of *sangria* to add an authentic Spanish flavor.

Serves 4

2 pints mussels, cleaned (see box, right)	1 onion, finely chopped
½ cup dry white wine	½ lb chorizo sausage, roughly chopped
2 garlic cloves, finely chopped	8 skinless chicken thighs
A few sprigs flat-leaf parsley	2–3 cups chicken stock
Salt and freshly ground pepper	2 cups arborio rice
3 tbs virgin olive oil	Large pinch saffron threads

CLEANING MUSSELS

It is important to clean mussels thoroughly before cooking. When you get them home, keep them in a bowl of cold water until ready to use, discarding any that are open or that do not close when tapped sharply against the edge of the bowl or the work surface. To clean mussels, hold them one at a time under cold running water and scrape off the stringy beards and any barnacles with a small sharp knife, then scrub the shells with a stiff brush to remove any weeds or sand still remaining. After cooking, check to see if all the mussels are open. Discard any mussels that are closed, because these will not be safe to eat.

1 Put the mussels in a pan with the wine, garlic, parsley, and salt and pepper to taste. Cover and bring to a boil, then simmer for 5 minutes or until the mussels open, shaking the pan frequently. Strain the mussels and set aside. Reserve the cooking liquid.

2 Heat the oil in a large paella pan or skillet, add the onion and chorizo, and sauté gently for 5 minutes. Add the chicken and sauté for about 10 minutes, until golden on all sides. Then add the mussel cooking liquid and 2 cups stock and bring to a boil.

3 Add the rice and saffron and simmer for 20 minutes or until both chicken and rice are tender, stirring frequently and adding more stock as necessary. Place the mussels on top of the rice, cover, and heat through. Taste for seasoning. Serve hot.

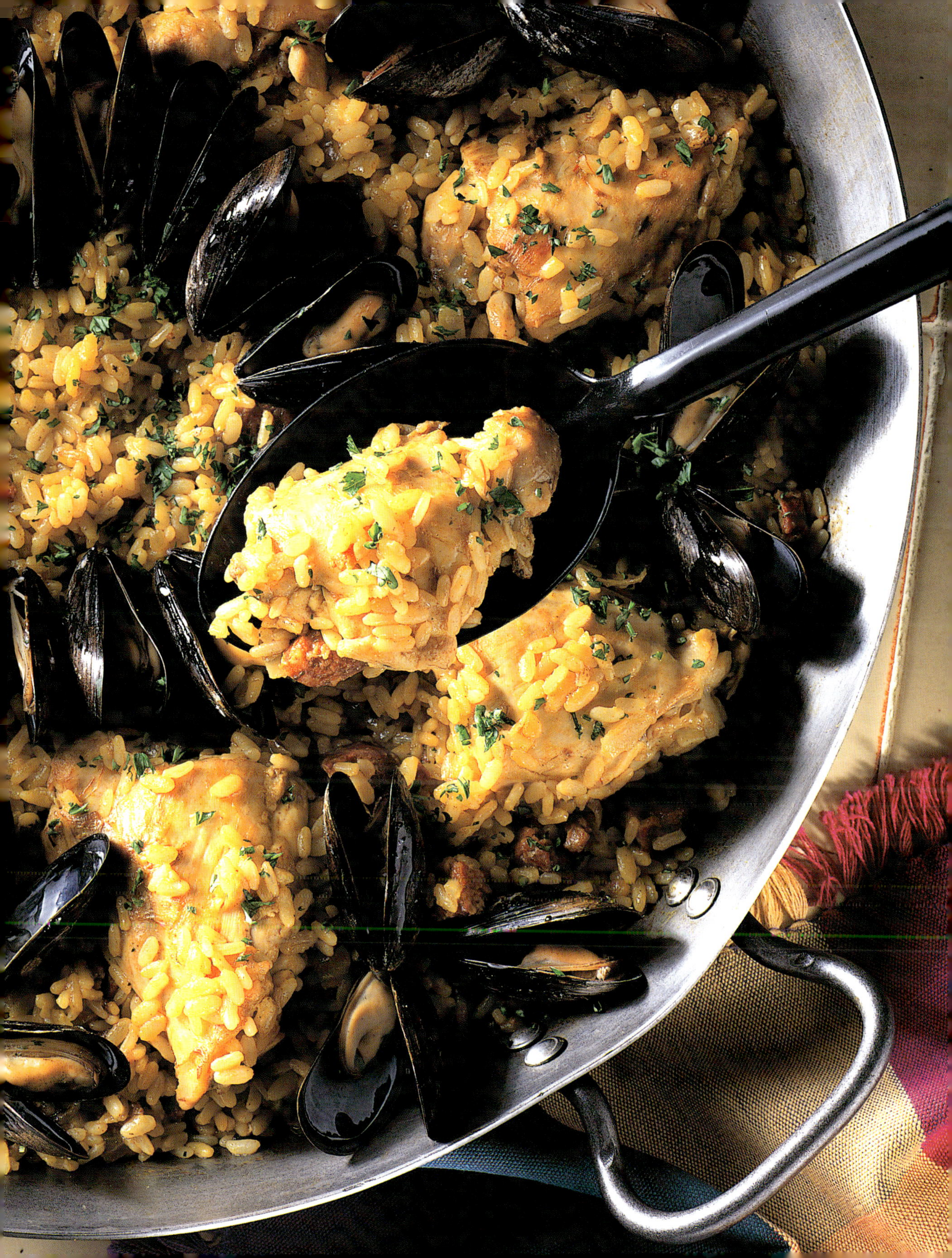

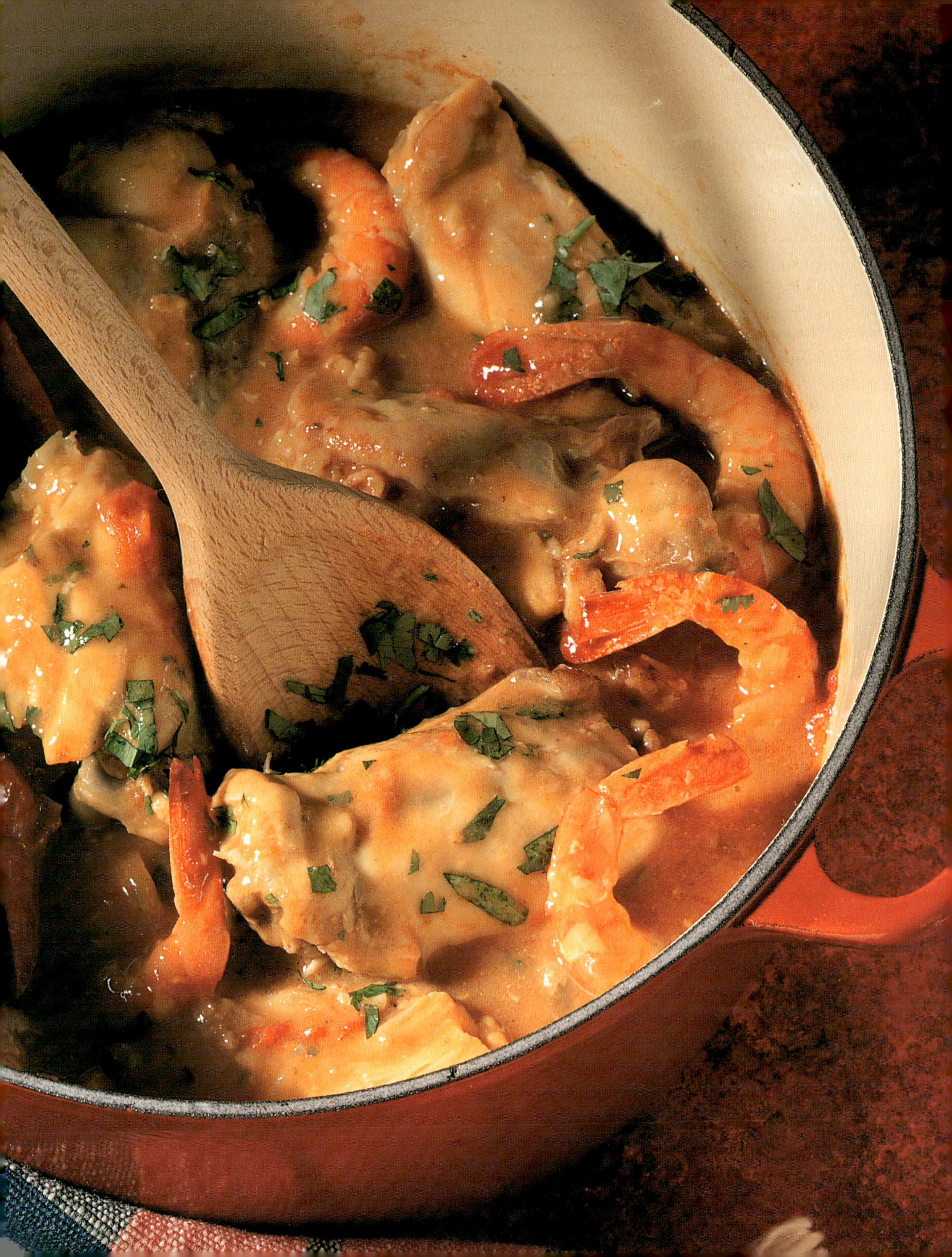

CHICKEN MARENGO

Shrimp and chicken are a winning combination. Here they're teamed in a rich red sauce and given exciting new flavor with the addition of spicy fresh coriander. Serve this with garlic mashed potatoes for a warming winter meal.

Serves 4

1 tb butter	14-oz can crushed tomatoes
2 tbs virgin olive oil	1 heaping tb tomato paste
1 onion, thinly sliced	1 tsp sugar
2 garlic cloves, minced	Salt and freshly ground pepper
12 chicken thighs, skinned	½ lb peeled cooked shrimp
2 tbs all-purpose flour	¼ cup chopped fresh coriander (cilantro)
1 cup dry white wine	

Finishing touches
Garnish each serving with a whole cooked shrimp in the shell.

MARENGO

Poulet à la Marengo *was created in 1800 for Napoleon Bonaparte after his victory over the Austrians at the battle of Marengo in northern Italy. The dish, prepared by Napoleon's chef Dunand on the battlefield, is said to have been made with pieces of chicken in a tomato, garlic, and brandy sauce, garnished with crayfish and fried eggs. The recipe here is a much simplified version, but is delicious nevertheless.*

The fresh coriander, although not strictly authentic, goes exceptionally well with the combination of chicken, tomatoes, and shrimp, but you can use flat-leaf parsley or chervil if you prefer.

---

1 Melt the butter with the oil in a large flameproof casserole, add the onion and garlic, and sauté gently until soft. Add the chicken and sprinkle with the flour, then sauté over moderate heat, turning the chicken constantly, until it is golden brown on all sides.

2 Add the wine, stir to loosen the browned bits from the pan, then add the tomatoes and bring to a boil, stirring. Lower the heat and add the tomato paste, sugar, and salt and pepper to taste. Cover and simmer for 40 minutes or until the chicken is tender.

3 Add the peeled cooked shrimp to the pan, stir well until coated in the sauce, and heat through for a few minutes. Remove the pan from the heat and stir in the coriander. Taste for seasoning. Serve hot, straight from the casserole.

BONELESS CHICKEN

Roasted Chicken and Vegetables

In this healthy, low-cholesterol dish, rosemary, garlic, and fruity olive oil capture the fabulous flavors of Provence. The roasted vegetables round out the dish, so no accompaniment is needed.

Serves 4

1 small red bell pepper	1 tb chopped fresh rosemary
1 small yellow bell pepper	Salt and freshly ground pepper
1 large whole head garlic	4 large skinless and boneless chicken breast halves
2 small zucchini	
1 lb small red potatoes	⅔ cup dry white wine
1 small eggplant	Fresh rosemary for garnish
¼ cup virgin olive oil	

ROSEMARY

This sweet-smelling, woody-tasting herb is used all over the Mediterranean. It has a natural affinity for meat and poultry, and is especially good with roast and grilled chicken and lamb. A favorite Provençal way of using rosemary is to put a few sprigs of the fresh herb under a bird or roast before cooking, or to use the twiggy stems of the herb instead of kebab skewers to thread chunks of meat and vegetables for grilling.

1 Cut the peppers into quarters lengthwise and discard the cores and seeds. Separate the garlic into cloves, removing the excess papery skin. Cut the zucchini, potatoes, and eggplant into chunks, leaving the skin on.

2 Put the vegetables in a roasting pan, sprinkle with the oil, chopped rosemary, and salt and pepper to taste, and turn to coat. Roast in a preheated 400°F oven for 40 minutes, turning the vegetables 2–3 times.

3 Add the chicken and roast for 20 minutes, turning once. Transfer the chicken to warmed plates. Put the pan on the top of the stove, add the wine, and stir over moderate heat. Spoon the vegetables over the chicken, garnish, and serve at once.

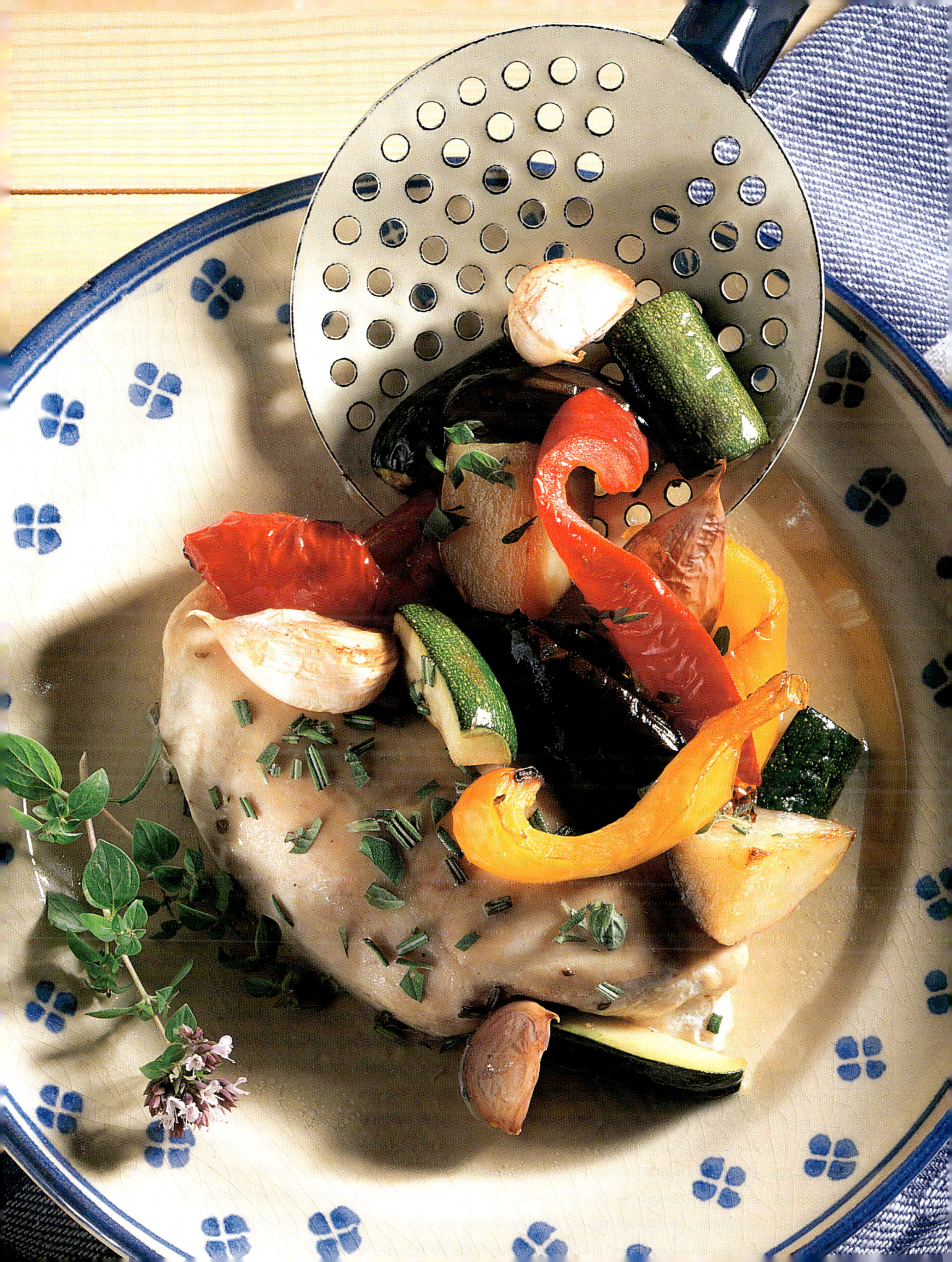

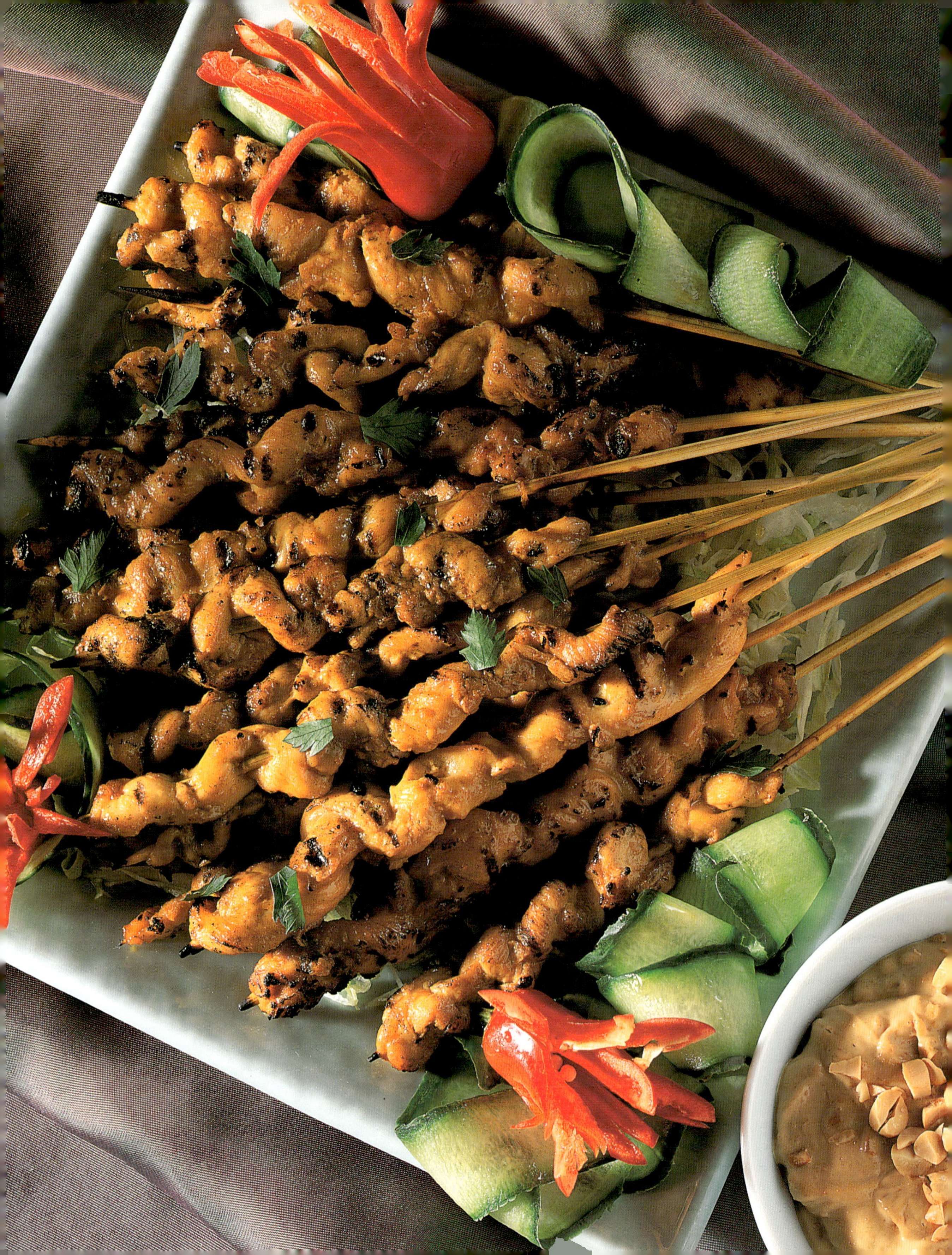

BONELESS CHICKEN

CHICKEN SATE

This Indonesian specialty – delicate chicken kebabs with a spicy coconut-flavor peanut dipping sauce – is easy to make at home. Be sure to use bamboo skewers for an authentic look. Saté makes excellent summer barbecue food and is equally good cooked under the broiler in winter.

PEANUT SAUCE

This is the traditional sauce served with saté in Indonesia. Gently heat 1 cup canned coconut milk in a pan with ¼ cup crunchy peanut butter, 2 minced garlic cloves, the juice of 1 lime, 1 tb soy sauce, 2 tsps sugar, and ½ tsp chili powder. Bring to a boil and simmer, stirring, for 3–5 minutes until thick. Let cool to room temperature. Stir well and sprinkle with chopped roasted peanuts before serving.

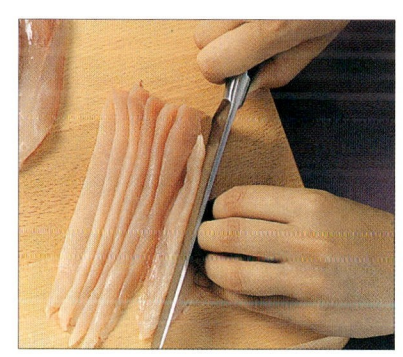

Serves 4–6

4 large skinless and boneless chicken breast halves	2 tsps sugar
1 small onion, grated	1 tsp turmeric
2 garlic cloves, minced	Shredded cucumber and red hot chili flowers for garnish
2 tbs soy sauce	
2 tbs canola oil	Peanut sauce (see box, right) for serving

1 Cut the chicken into 36 strips. Whisk together the remaining ingredients (except the garnish and peanut sauce) and pour over the chicken. Cover and marinate in the refrigerator overnight.

2 Soak 18 bamboo skewers in warm water for 30 minutes. Drain the skewers, then thread 2 chicken strips on each skewer, twisting the strips so they wind securely around the skewers.

3 Grill the chicken for about 5 minutes, turning once and brushing with the marinade from the dish. Serve hot, garnished with cucumber and chili flowers. Pass the peanut sauce separately.

Chicken Pinwheels

The simple technique of making pinwheels turns regular chicken breasts into something really special. They're perfect for entertaining because you can stuff, roll, and wrap them up to 24 hours in advance.

Spinach and Ricotta Pinwheels

Serves 4

½ lb fresh spinach leaves, washed

Salt and freshly ground pepper

¼ lb ricotta cheese

Large pinch grated nutmeg

4 large skinless and boneless chicken breast halves

12 slices bacon

1 cup red wine

1 Cook the spinach with 1 tsp salt for 5 minutes. Drain and let cool, then chop and squeeze to remove water. Mix with the ricotta, nutmeg, and pepper.

2 Cut and pound the chicken breasts (see box, right). Spread the spinach mixture over the chicken. Put 1 fillet along 1 long side of each chicken breast, and roll up the breast to enclose it.

3 Wrap each roll in 3 bacon slices, place in a roasting pan, and bake in a preheated 400°F oven for 30 minutes. Lift out the rolls, pour in the wine, and boil on top of the stove until reduced. Serve the chicken sliced, with the sauce drizzled over it.

Pancetta and Cheese Pinwheels

Serves 4

4 large skinless and boneless chicken breast halves

Salt and freshly ground pepper

4 thin slices Fontina or Gruyère cheese, total weight about ¼ lb

⅓ cup chopped sun-dried tomatoes

8 large fresh basil leaves

12 slices pancetta

1 cup red wine

1 Cut and pound the chicken breasts (see box, right). Season the cut side of each breast with salt and pepper, then cover with 1 slice of cheese.

2 Scatter the tomatoes over the cheese. Put 1 fillet along 1 long side of each chicken breast, tuck in 2 basil leaves, and roll up to enclose the filling.

3 Wrap each roll in 3 pancetta slices, place in a roasting pan, and bake in a preheated 400°F oven for 30 minutes. Lift out the rolls, pour in the wine, and boil on top of the stove until reduced. Serve the chicken sliced, with the sauce drizzled over it.

Preparing Chicken for Pinwheels

Before rolling it up, the chicken needs to be cut and pounded.

Make a horizontal slit through each chicken breast half without cutting all the way through. Reserve the chicken fillets.

Open out the chicken and place cut-side-up between 2 sheets of waxed paper. Flatten the meat by pounding it gently with a rolling pin or meat mallet.

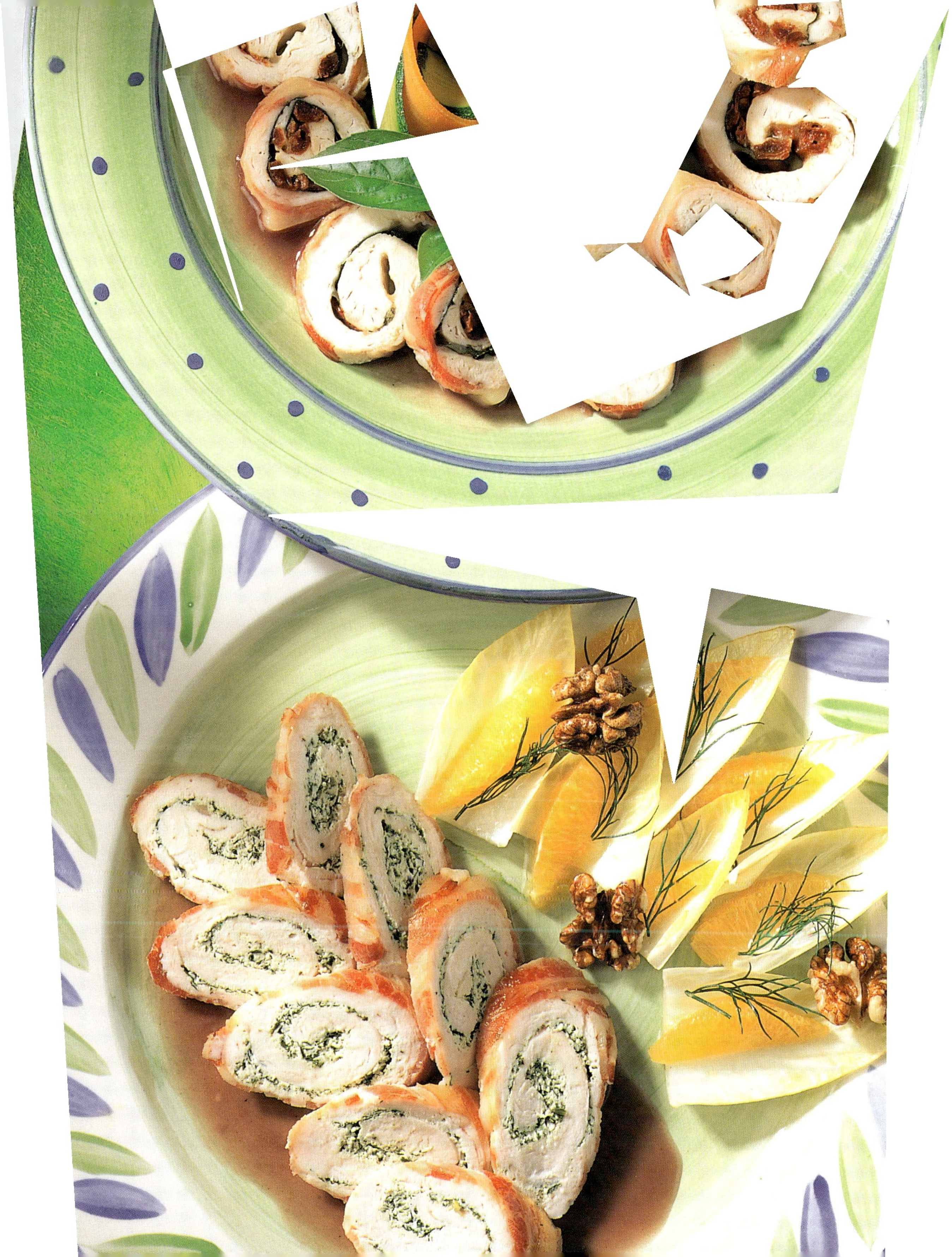

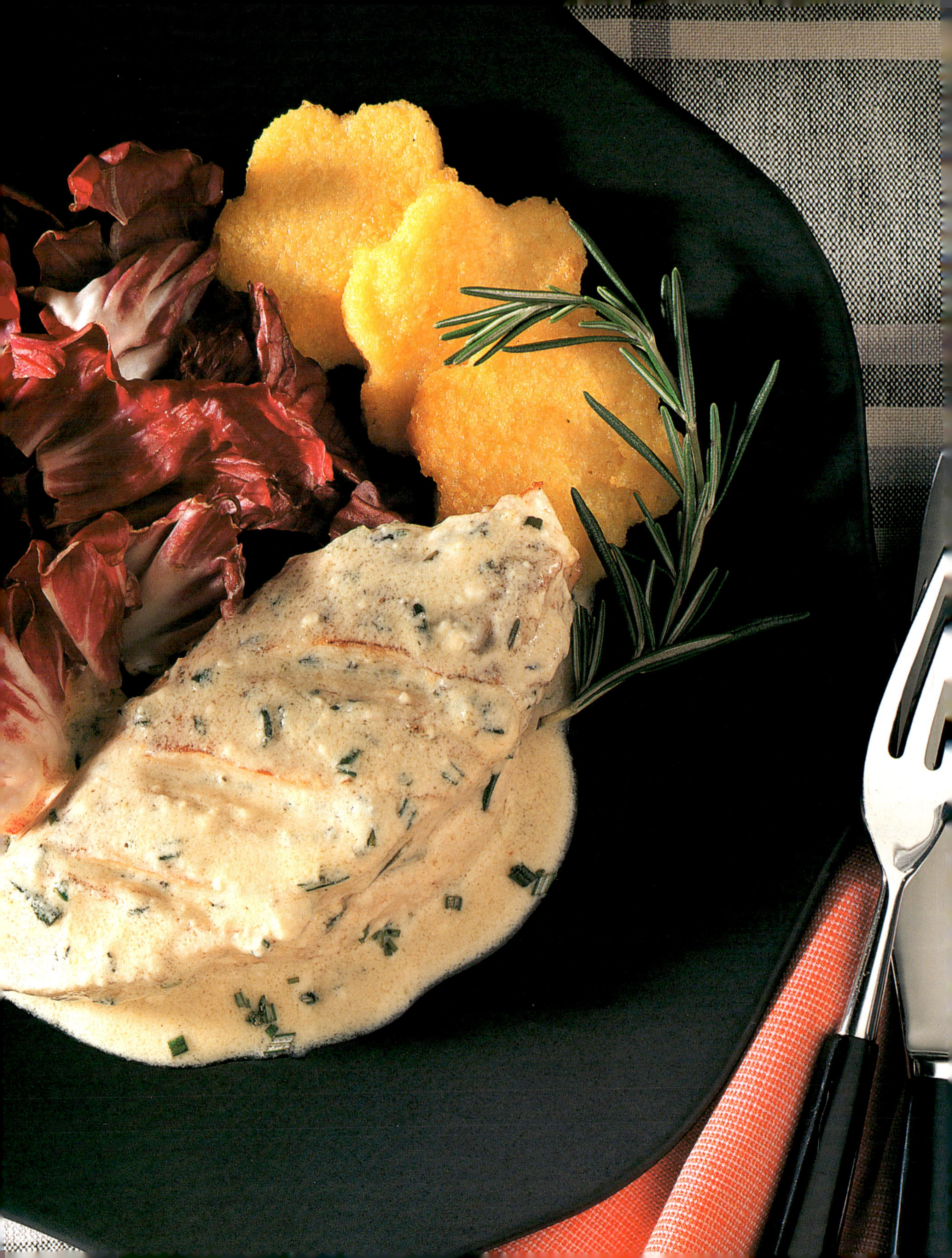

BONELESS CHICKEN

Chicken with Mascarpone

Melted mascarpone cheese makes a rich, creamy sauce in seconds. Here it's combined with Marsala and fresh rosemary for instant Italian flavor.

Serves 4

4 large skinless and boneless chicken breast halves	1 tb butter
2 tbs virgin olive oil	6 tbs Marsala
Finely grated zest and juice of 1 lemon	⅓ cup mascarpone cheese
1½ tbs finely chopped fresh rosemary	Fresh rosemary sprigs for garnish
Salt and freshly ground pepper	Fried polenta for serving (see box, right)

FRIED POLENTA

The striking color of fried polenta makes it a good accompaniment for pale, creamy sauces, and the crispness gives a good contrast in texture. The polenta can be made and cut into shapes up to 4 hours ahead, but should be fried just before serving. Bring 3 cups water to a boil in a large pan, add 1 tsp salt, and 1 cup pre-cooked cornmeal. Simmer for 8 minutes, stirring, until very thick, then pour onto an oiled baking sheet. Let cool, then cut into shapes with a cookie cutter, and fry in about 3 tbs hot virgin olive oil for 2–3 minutes on each side until crisp. Drain on paper towels before serving.

---

1 Make 3 diagonal slashes in the fleshy side of each chicken breast. Place the chicken in a dish and add the oil, lemon zest and juice, 1 tb rosemary, and salt and pepper to taste. Turn the chicken to coat, then cover and marinate for at least 1 hour.

2 Melt the butter in a skillet, add the chicken, reserving the marinade, and sauté over moderate heat for 5 minutes. Add the marinade, Marsala, and ¼ cup water. Simmer for 20 minutes or until the chicken is tender. Transfer the chicken to warmed plates.

3 Boil the cooking juices until reduced, add the mascarpone and the remaining rosemary, and simmer until thickened. Taste for seasoning. Spoon the sauce over the chicken, garnish, and serve at once with the fried polenta.

Simple Chicken Curries

Chicken is excellent for curries because it quickly picks up the flavor of the spices. As with all spicy dishes, the flavor of these curries improves when they are chilled and reheated the next day. Ghee is clarified butter.

Chicken Pasanda

Serves 4

3 tbs ghee or butter

1 onion, thinly sliced

2 garlic cloves, finely chopped

2-inch piece fresh ginger root, peeled and minced

2 tbs ground coriander

1 tsp turmeric

2 lbs skinless and boneless chicken thighs and breasts, cubed

½ cup heavy cream

1 tsp salt

⅓ cup toasted sliced almonds

Fresh coriander (cilantro) for garnish

1 Melt the ghee or butter in a pan, add the onion, garlic, ginger, spices, and sauté gently for 5 minutes.

2 Add the thigh meat, cream, salt, half the almonds, and ½ cup water, and stir well to combine. Cover, and simmer gently for 20 minutes.

3 Add the breast meat and simmer for 20 minutes. Garnish with the remaining almonds and the fresh coriander before serving.

Kashmiri Chicken

Serves 4

3 tbs ghee or butter

1 large onion, finely chopped

2 garlic cloves, finely chopped

2 tbs curry powder

1 tb paprika

1 tsp chili powder

2 lbs skinless and boneless chicken thighs and breasts, cubed

1 cup plain yogurt

6 tomatoes, skinned and chopped

1 tsp salt

¼ cup chopped fresh mint

1 Melt the ghee or butter in a pan, add the onion, garlic, and spices, and sauté gently for 5 minutes. Add the thigh meat and stir to coat with the spice mixture.

2 Add half the yogurt, a little at a time, and stir-fry until it is all absorbed. Add the tomatoes, ½ cup water, and the salt. Cover, and simmer gently for 20 minutes.

3 Add the breast meat, simmer for 20 minutes, then stir in half the mint. Garnish with the remaining yogurt and mint before serving.

Chicken Siam

Serves 4

2 14-oz cans coconut milk

2 tbs Thai green curry paste

1½ lbs skinless and boneless chicken breast meat, cubed

2 tbs Thai fish sauce

2 tsps sugar

½ cup pea eggplant or diced unpeeled eggplant

½ cup finely diced green beans

Kaffir lime leaves for garnish

1 Spoon the cream off the top of the coconut milk, put the cream in a wok, and bring to a boil. Add the curry paste and stir-fry until the oil separates.

2 Add the chicken and turn to coat in the sauce. Simmer for 5–7 minutes until tender, adding the coconut milk a few spoonfuls at a time.

3 Add the fish sauce, sugar, eggplant, and beans and stir-fry for 2–3 minutes or until tender. Garnish with kaffir lime leaves before serving.

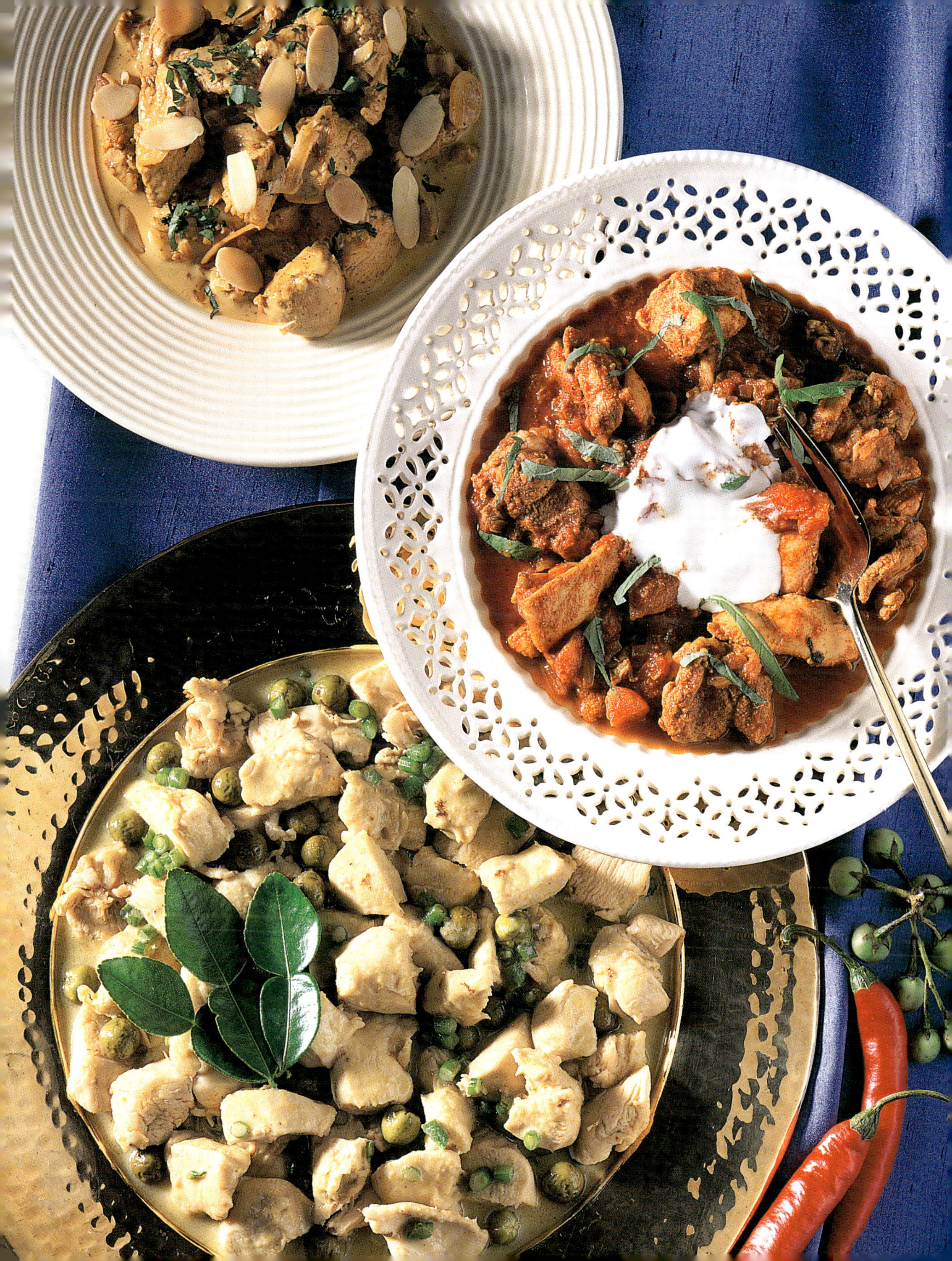

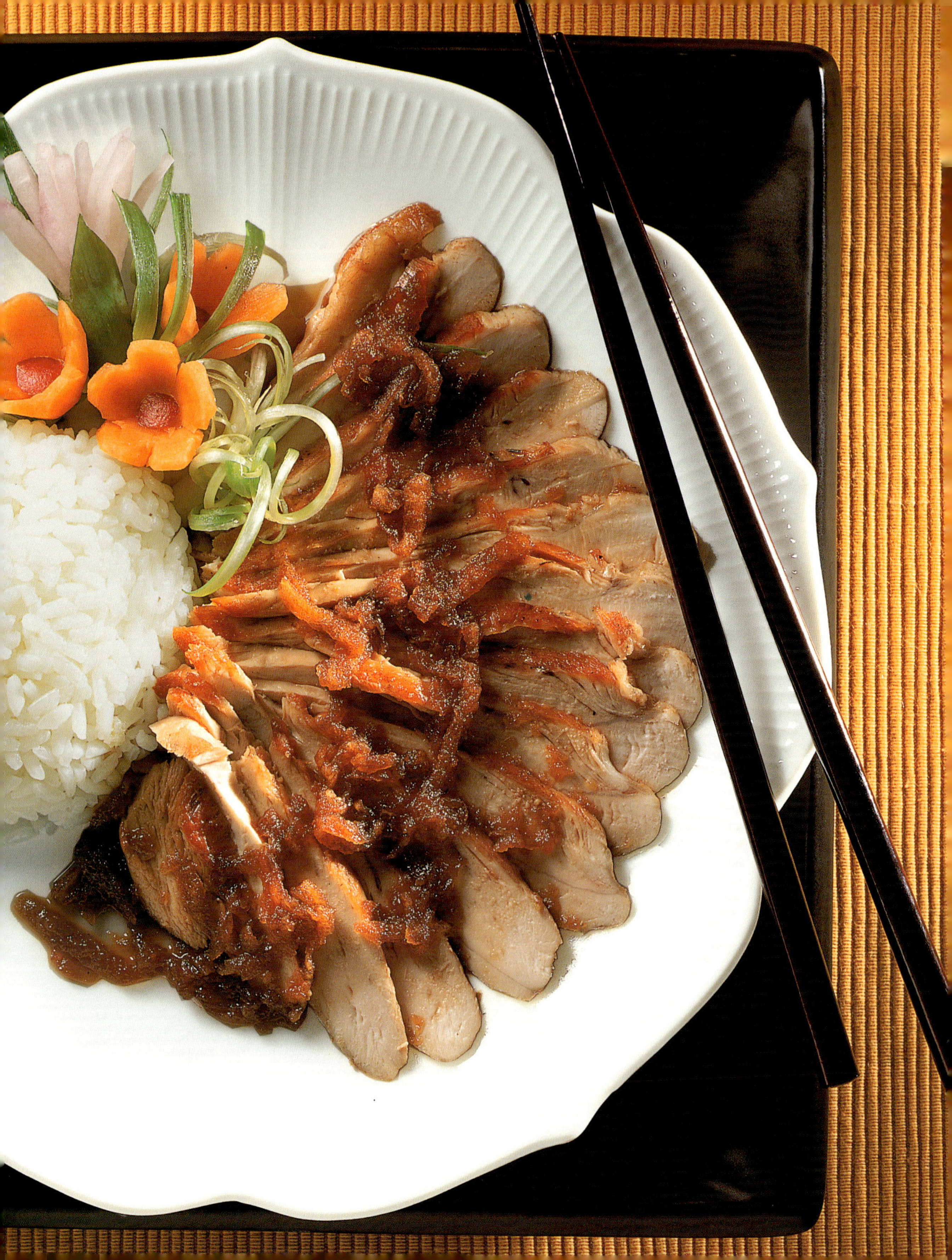

BONELESS CHICKEN

Teriyaki Chicken

This Japanese-style dish is incredibly quick and easy, and the sauce can be used with other meats as well – beef fillet and pork tenderloin are also very good cooked teriyaki-style.

Serves 4

¼ cup Japanese soy sauce (shoyu)	4 large skinless and boneless chicken breast halves
¼ cup Japanese rice wine (sake)	
2 tbs Japanese sweet rice wine (mirin)	1 Golden Delicious apple, peeled, cored, and grated
1 tb sugar	Steamed Japanese white rice for serving
2 tbs canola oil	

Special touches
Garnish each serving with scallion, radish, and carrot flowers.

> ### JAPANESE INGREDIENTS
> *These are easy to find at large supermarkets and Asian stores.* **Shoyu** *is naturally fermented soy sauce. There are two kinds – light and dark. Most Japanese cooks use the dark soy sauce for general cooking purposes and the light only when cooking a light-colored dish.* **Sake** *is colorless rice wine made from fermented steamed rice. It is a very popular drink in Japan. There are many different qualities; use an inexpensive one for cooking.* **Mirin** *is sweetened rice wine with a low alcohol content. It is used extensively in Japanese cooking, but never served as a drink as sake is.*

1 Gently heat the soy sauce, rice wines, and sugar in a pan until the sugar has dissolved. Put the chicken in a preheated, lightly oiled, cast-iron pan and cook for 1–2 minutes on each side, pressing with a spatula to keep it flat. Pour the sauce over the chicken.

2 Add the grated apple and stir well to mix. Cook over gentle heat for 5 minutes or until the chicken is tender when pierced. Turn the chicken over and baste with the sauce several times during cooking. Remove the chicken with a slotted spoon.

3 Cut the chicken on the diagonal into very thin slices and fan out the slices on warmed plates. Boil the sauce until it has reduced slightly, then spoon it over the chicken. Serve at once, with steamed rice.

BONELESS CHICKEN

Chicken en Papillote

Paper parcels enclose tender juicy chicken topped with finely cut ratatouille vegetables to make a low-fat main dish packed with Provençal flavor. Serve this with new potatoes tossed with chopped fresh chives.

Serves 4

¼ cup virgin olive oil	2 ripe tomatoes, finely diced
1 small onion, thinly sliced	¼ cup dry white wine
1 garlic clove, minced	½ tsp herbes de Provence
1 small yellow pepper, cored, seeded, and cut into julienne	Salt and freshly ground pepper
1 zucchini, cut into julienne	4 large skinless and boneless chicken breast halves

Seasonal choice
Use 1 tb chopped fresh herbs, such as basil, sage, summer savory, and thyme, instead of the herbes de Provence.

> ### EN PAPILLOTE
> *This is the French term for baking food wrapped in paper. Either baking parchment or aluminum foil can be used. Both are equally successful at protecting the food and helping to retain its natural moisture and juiciness, but paper is preferable for presentation at the table. When the parcel is in the oven, it holds the steam produced by the food as it cooks and puffs up attractively. To maximize the effect of baking in parchment, bring the parcels to the table unopened, allowing each diner to cut open the top. For an even more decorative presentation, cut heart-shaped pieces of baking parchment instead of rounds.*

1 Heat 3 tbs oil in a skillet, add the vegetables, and sauté for about 5 minutes. Add half the wine, the herbs, and salt and pepper to taste. Simmer uncovered, stirring frequently, for 10 minutes or until softened.

2 Cut out 4 rounds of baking parchment, each 12 inches in diameter. Brush 1 side of each round with oil. Put 1 chicken breast half on each round, slightly off center. Spoon some of the vegetables on top of the chicken and moisten with the pan juices.

3 Fold the baking parchment over the chicken, twist the curved edges together to seal, and twist the ends tightly. Place the parcels on a baking sheet and bake in a preheated 400°F oven for 20 minutes. Serve at once, with the remaining vegetables.

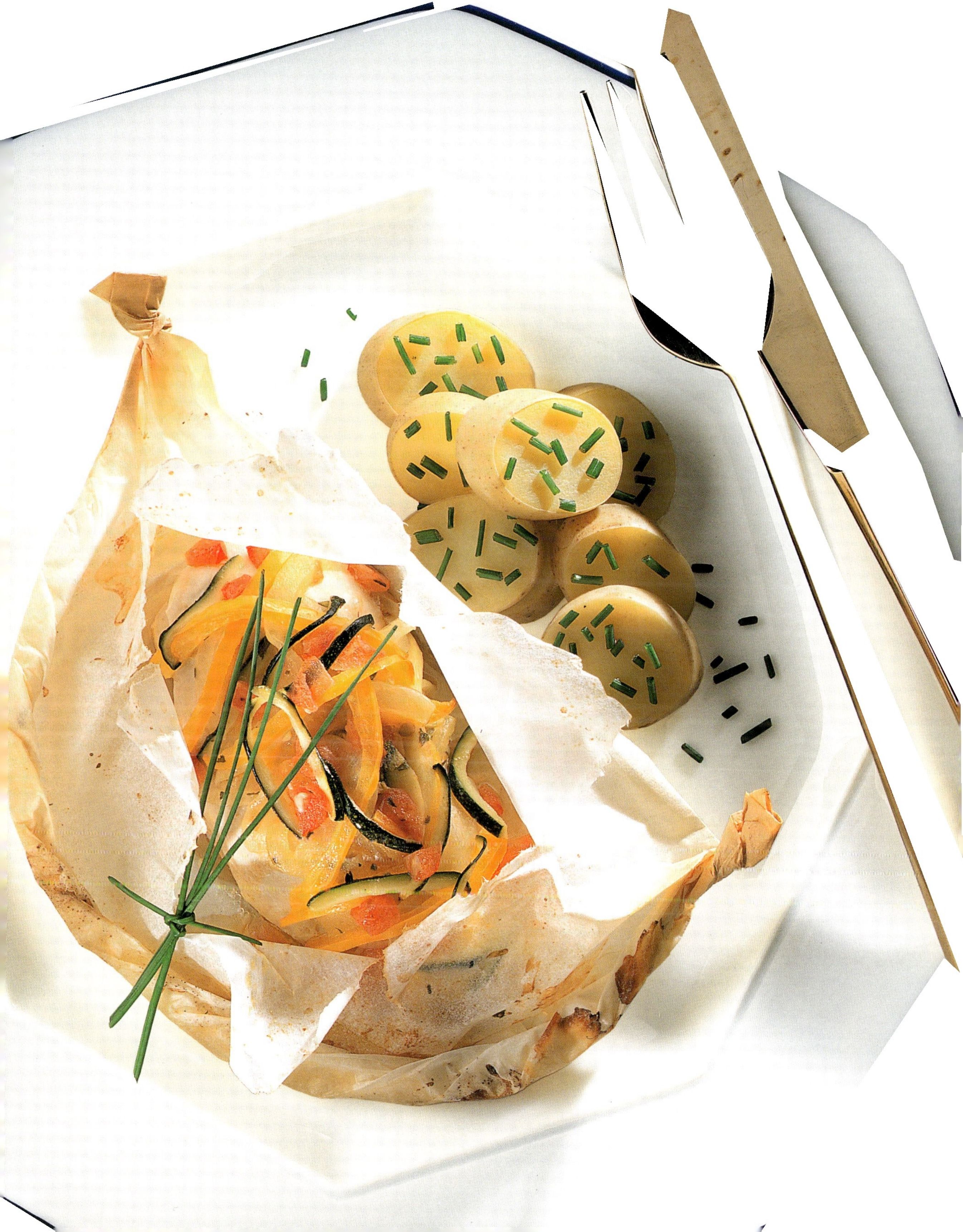

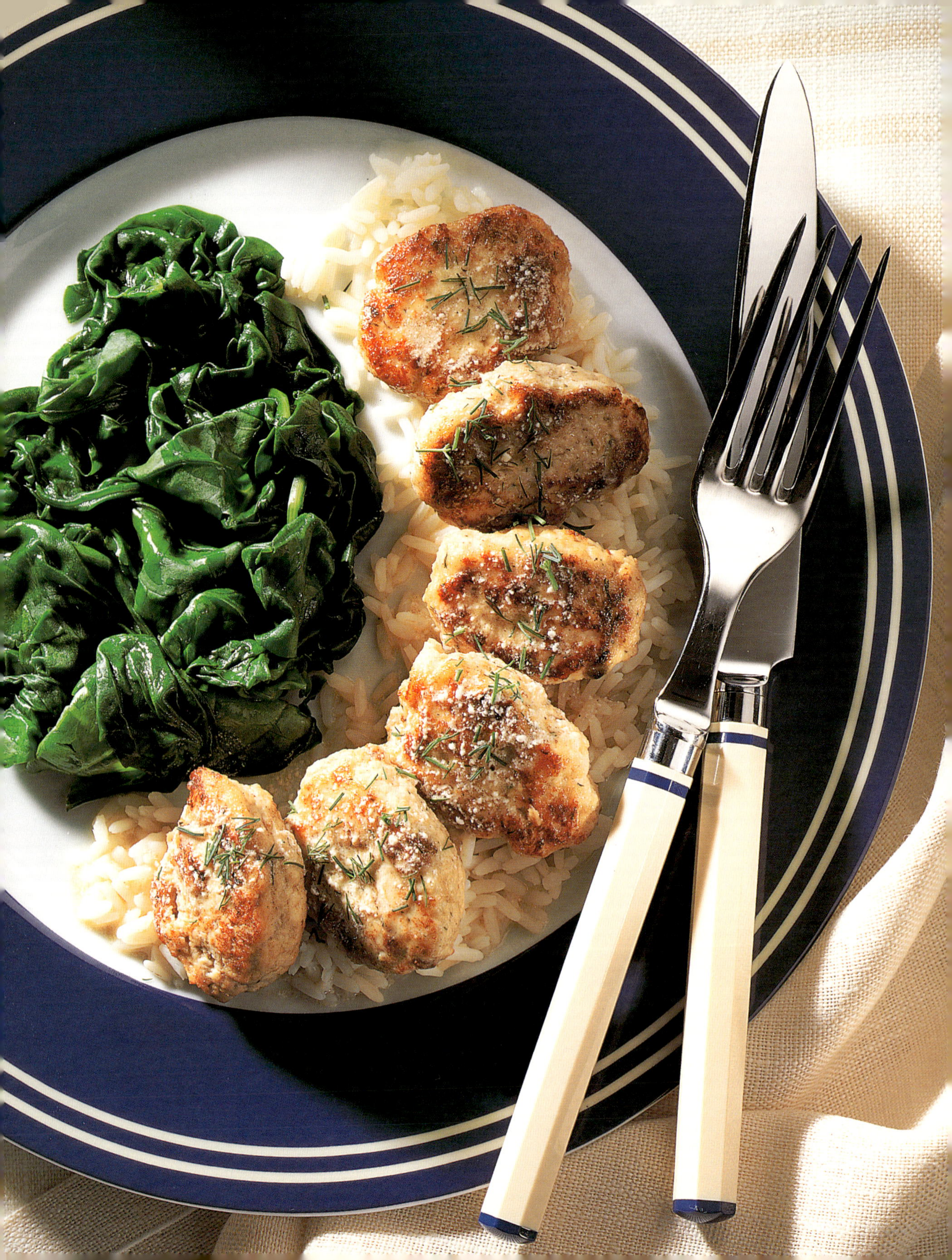

FRIKADELLER

These tasty meatballs come from Denmark, where they are traditionally served with boiled white rice and ice-cold Danish beer. Lightly cooked spinach is served alongside for a nutritious and substantial meal.

Serves 4–6

1 lb skinless and boneless chicken breast meat, sliced	Salt and freshly ground pepper
1 small onion, roughly chopped	1 tb butter
2 thick slices crustless wholewheat bread, torn into pieces	2 tbs canola oil
	1 cup dry white wine
Finely grated zest and juice of 1 lemon	½ cup chicken stock
¼ cup chopped fresh dill	¼ cup sour cream

FRIKADELLER

This is the Danish word for fried meatballs, one of Denmark's most popular dishes, the equivalent of burgers for us. Every cook in Denmark has his or her own version of frikadeller, which are traditionally made of ground pork or a mixture of ground pork and beef or ground pork and veal, sometimes with spice added. This chicken version is lighter and less fatty, and therefore more healthy, and the addition of fresh dill gives a touch of freshness to the overall flavor. Danish cooks often use 2 soup spoons to make the meat mixture into the traditional torpedo shape, but this can be a little tricky if you haven't had practice.

1 Work the chicken in a food processor with the onion, bread, lemon zest, half the dill, 1 tsp salt, and plenty of pepper. Do not overwork or the chicken will be rubbery. Turn the mixture out of the machine and shape into 24 ovals with wet hands.

2 Melt the butter with the oil in a large skillet. Add half the meatballs and fry over moderate heat for 5 minutes or until golden on all sides. Remove with a slotted spoon and drain on paper towels. Repeat with the remaining meatballs.

3 Stir the wine, stock, and lemon juice into the skillet and bring to a boil. Add the meatballs and salt and pepper to taste and simmer for 10 minutes. Remove from the heat, add the sour cream, and shake the pan. Serve hot, with the remaining dill.

BONELESS CHICKEN

WARM CHICKEN SALAD

Pretty salad leaves, asparagus spears, and chicken make this a substantial main-dish salad. The warm dressing of olive oil and raspberry vinegar softens the curly and crispy leaves and adds a fresh, fruity touch.

Serves 4

¼ cup virgin olive oil	1 small head radicchio, torn into small pieces
4 large skinless and boneless chicken breast halves, cut into thin strips	½ head frisée, torn into small pieces
¼ cup sun-dried tomatoes in olive oil, thinly sliced	½ lb asparagus spears, each one cut into thirds
1 garlic clove, minced	2 tbs raspberry vinegar (see box, right)
Salt and freshly ground pepper	½ tsp sugar

RASPBERRY VINEGAR

Available in bottles at large supermarkets, this fruity wine vinegar is absolutely delicious in dressings for salads, going especially well with the flavor of sun-dried tomatoes. It's also very good for deglazing pan juices after cooking chicken or meat, so always keep a bottle handy in your pantry. Buy the best quality available and you will find that a little goes a long way.

1 Heat 2 tbs oil in a non-stick frying pan, add the chicken, tomatoes, garlic, and salt and pepper to taste, and stir-fry for 5 minutes or until the chicken is tender. Put salad leaves in a bowl.

2 Remove the chicken with a slotted spoon and place on top of the salad leaves. Add the asparagus to the pan and stir-fry for 1–2 minutes. Remove and add to the chicken.

3 Whisk together the remaining oil, the vinegar, and sugar, and pour into the pan. Stir over high heat until hot, then pour over the salad and toss quickly to combine. Serve at once.

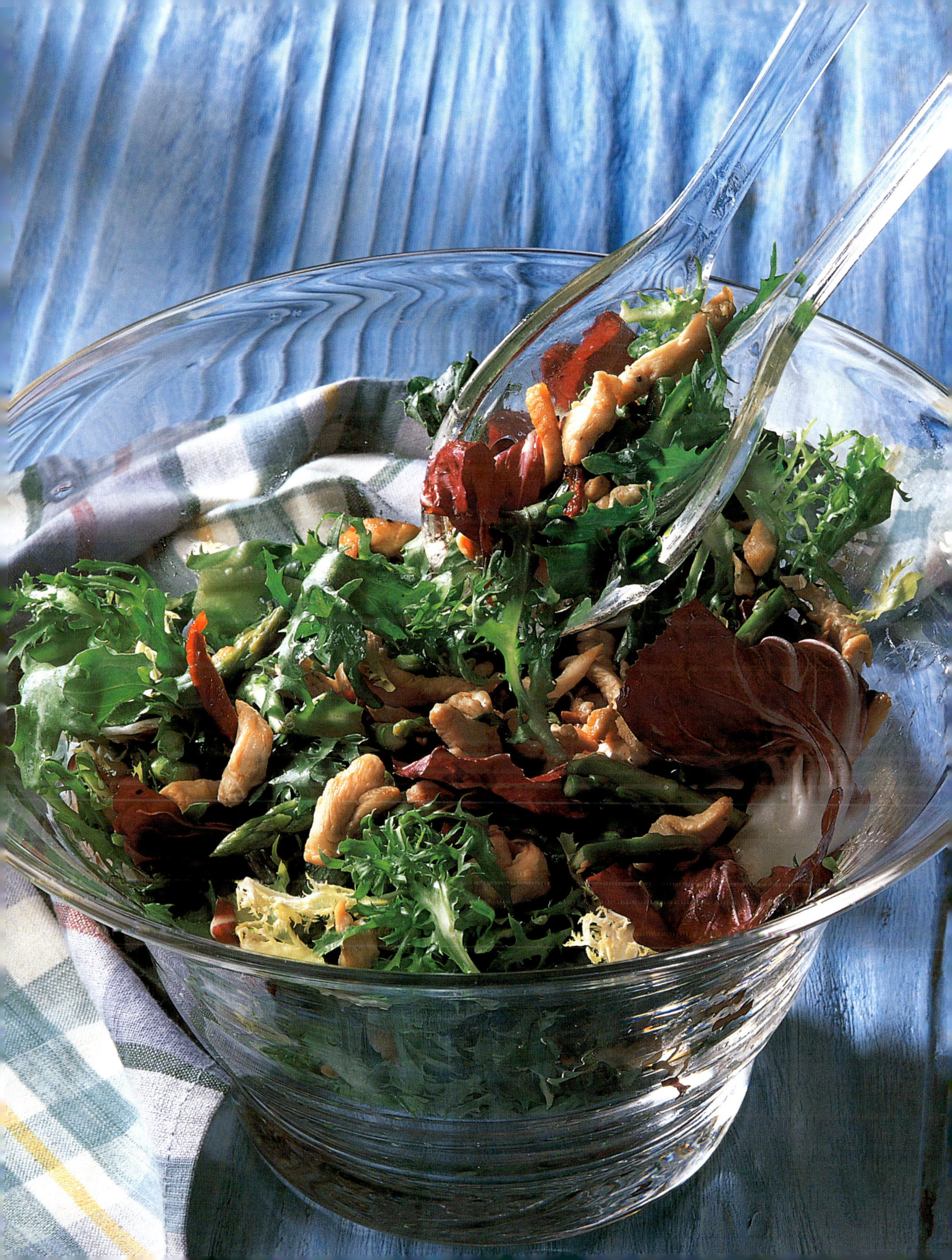

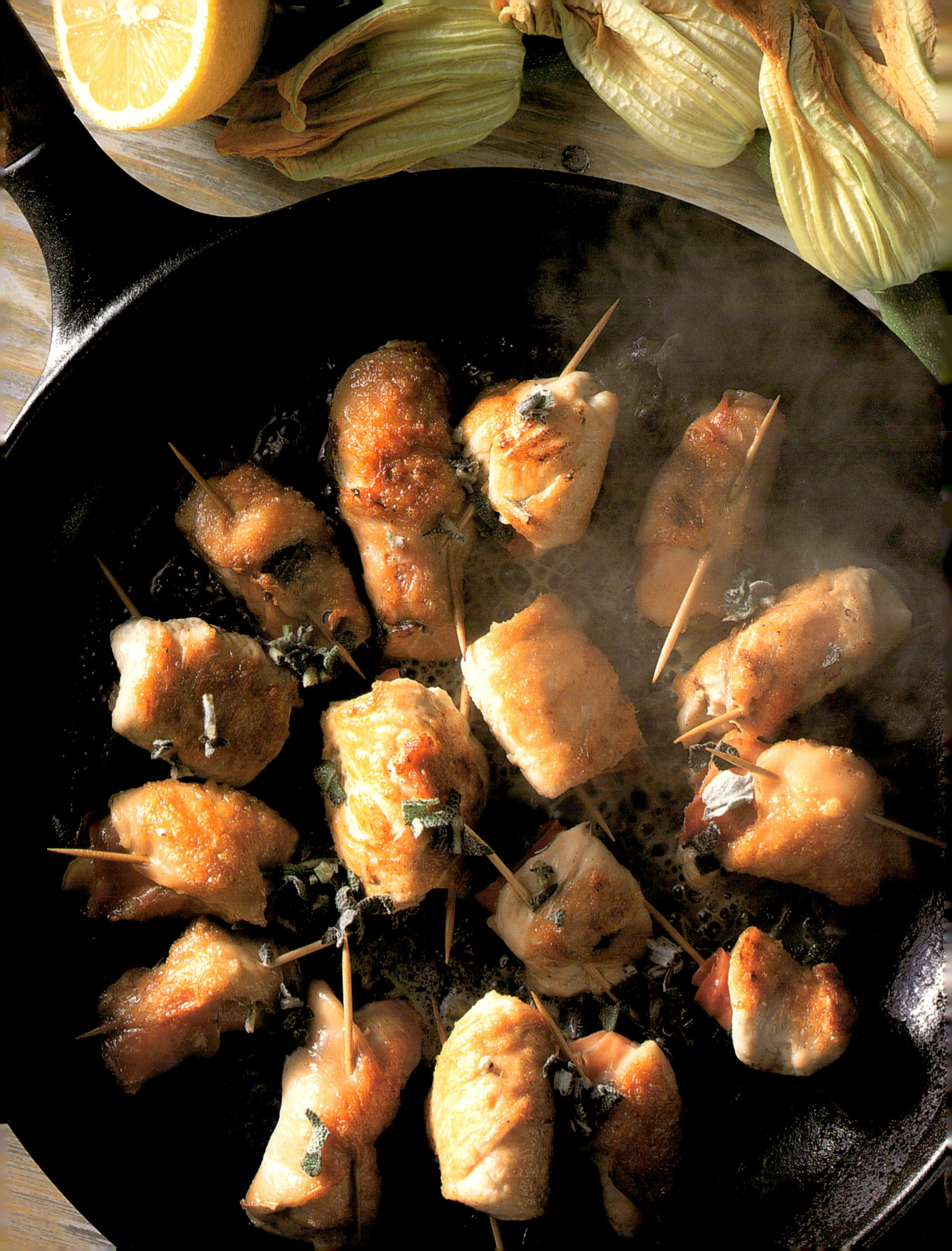

BONELESS CHICKEN

SALTIMBOCCA

Amazingly quick and easy to make, this rolled chicken is literally bursting with Italian flavor. Serve it for an impromptu dinner with sliced zucchini, sautéed potatoes, and a bottle of chilled dry white wine.

Serves 4

4 large skinless and boneless chicken breast halves	1 tb virgin olive oil
Freshly ground pepper	½ cup dry white wine
16 fresh sage leaves	1–2 tbs chopped fresh sage
¼ lb very thinly sliced prosciutto	
2 tbs butter	

Finishing touches
Serve with lemon wedges for squeezing, and remove the toothpicks if you like.

SALTIMBOCCA

This Italian word means "jump into the mouth." The story goes that the name was given to the dish because it was so delicious it literally jumped out of the pan into the mouth of the hungry diner. The original recipe comes from Rome, where it is usually made with veal scallopine or beef fillet. Good-quality prosciutto and fresh sage are essential ingredients. The wine can be replaced by Marsala if preferred.

---

1 Cut each chicken breast half diagonally into 4 pieces. Put the chicken pieces, including the fillets, between 2 sheets of waxed paper and flatten them by pounding with a rolling pin.

2 Sprinkle the pieces of chicken liberally with pepper and place 1 sage leaf on each. Top with a piece of prosciutto, roll up, and secure each roll with a wooden toothpick.

3 Melt the butter with the oil in a large skillet. Add the chicken and sauté over high heat for 3–4 minutes. Add the wine and shake the pan vigorously. Sprinkle with the chopped sage and serve at once.

BONELESS CHICKEN

Sauteed Chicken Sandwich with Bacon

This sandwich is made with Italian ciabatta, sizzling hot chicken, and crisp bacon. Packed with baby salad greens, tomato, and horseradish mayonnaise, it makes the perfect lunch.

Serves 2

1 ciabatta loaf (see box, right)	1 small skinless and boneless chicken breast half
¼ cup mayonnaise	
1–2 tsps horseradish, to taste	4 slices bacon
1–2 ripe plum tomatoes, thinly sliced	1 handful baby salad greens
Salt and freshly ground pepper	

CIABATTA

This open-textured Italian bread is available at most shops selling fresh European-style breads and at some large supermarkets. Made with olive oil, it has a full flavor, chewy texture, and crisp crust. The open crumb of ciabatta and its flat shape – it takes its name from the Italian word for slipper – makes it perfect for sandwiches because it is not too "bready." Plain ciabatta can be used or, for extra flavor, you could try sun-dried tomato ciabatta or black olive ciabatta, both of which may be a bit more difficult to find, but well worth the effort. Once sliced in half, but before spreading it with the mayonnaise, the bread may be toasted; it crisps nicely.

---

1 Cut the loaf in half horizontally. Mix the mayonnaise and horseradish together and spread over the cut sides of the bread. Arrange the tomato slices along 1 of the ciabatta halves and sprinkle with salt and pepper.

2 Cut the chicken in half horizontally. Put the chicken, including the fillet, between 2 sheets of waxed paper and flatten by pounding with a rolling pin. Cook the bacon in a non-stick skillet until crisp. Drain on paper towels.

3 Add the chicken and cook for 2–3 minutes on each side until tender, pressing to keep it flat. Put the chicken and bacon on top of the tomato and cover with salad greens. Close the sandwich, cut it in half, and serve at once.

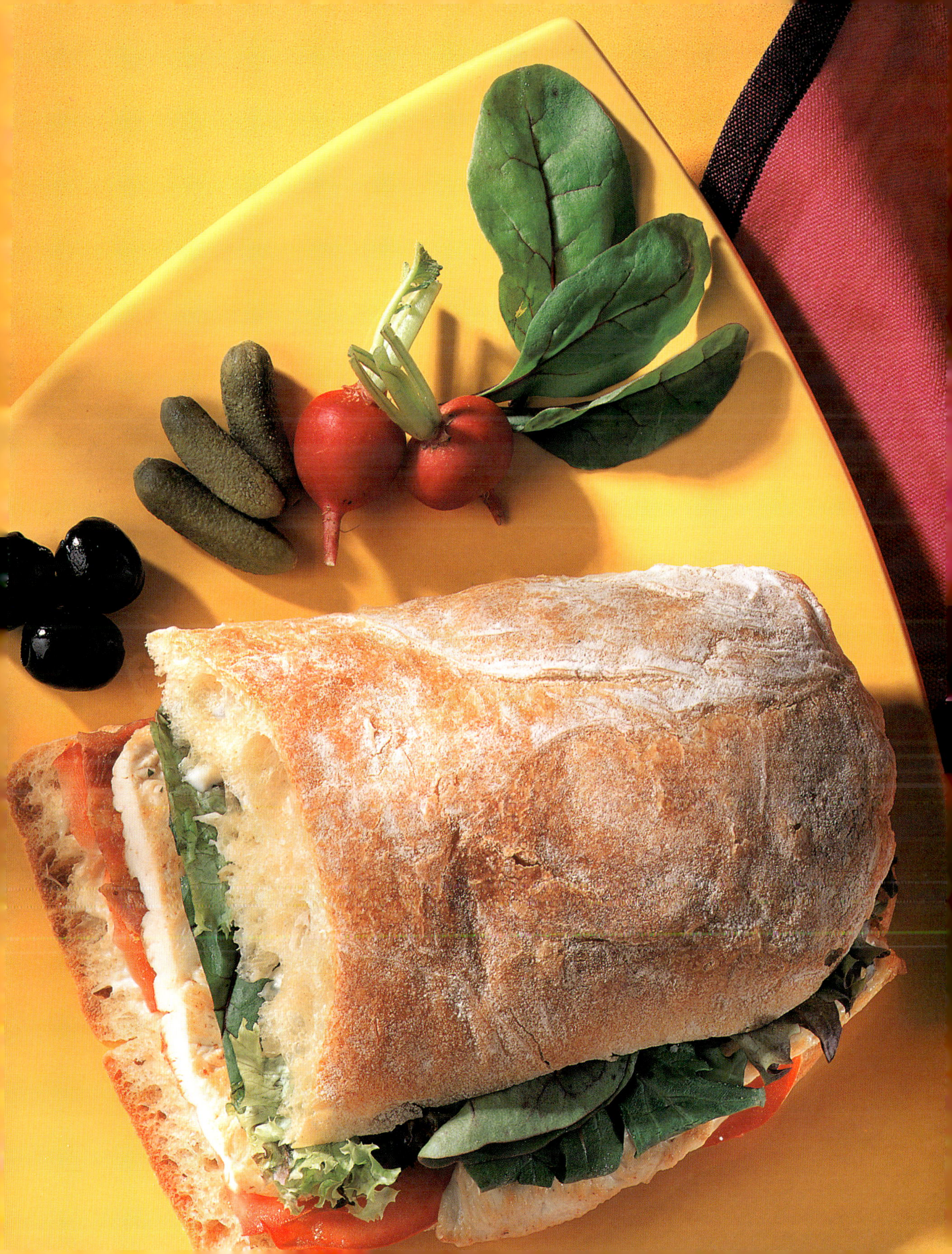

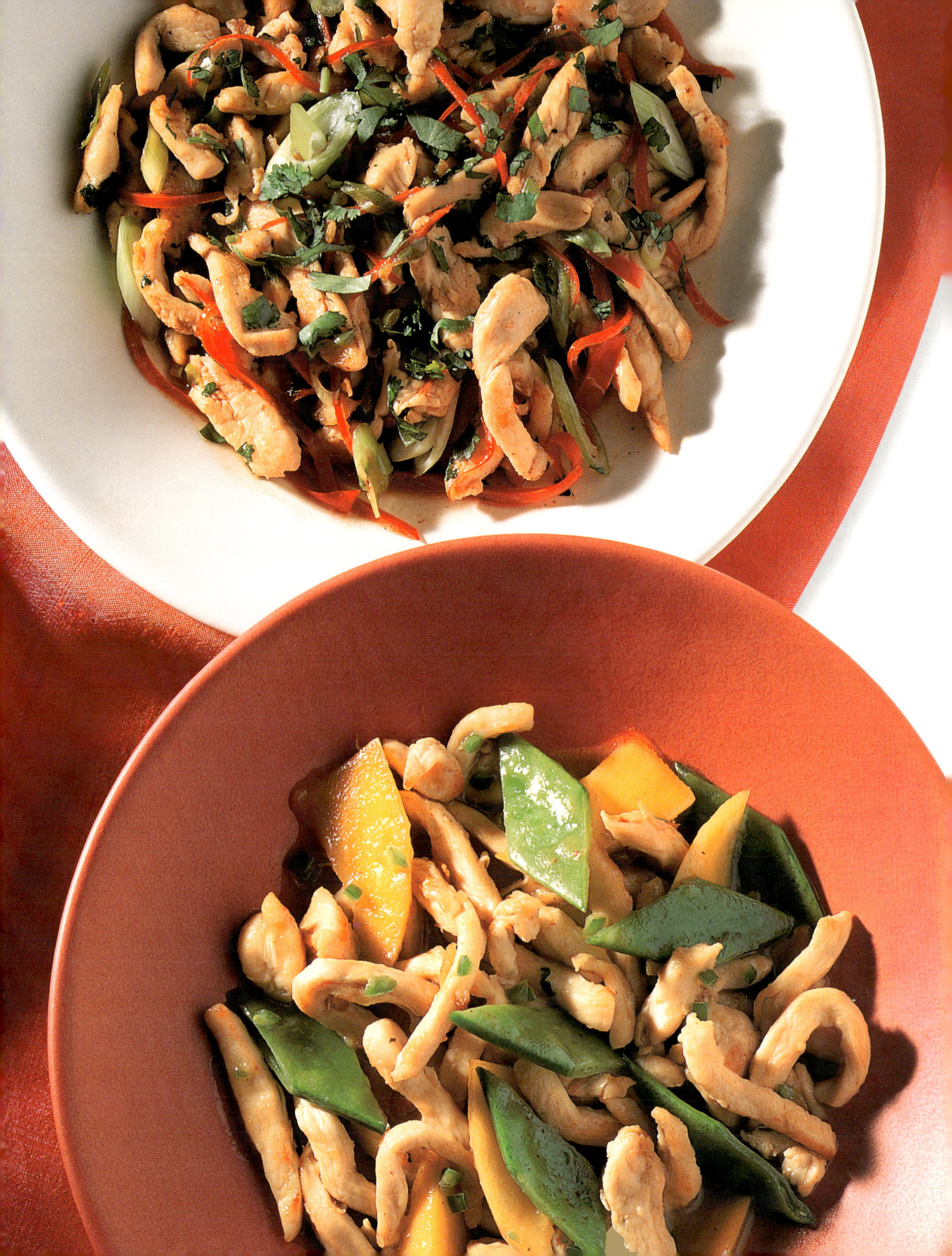

ASIAN STIR-FRIES

Stir-fries are quick and easy, and very healthy. These recipes use a combination of chicken and fruit, so popular in Asia, that makes them both fresh and light. Serve these with boiled rice or noodles.

CHINESE CHICKEN

Serves 4

4 tsps cornstarch
¼ cup soy sauce, or more to taste
2 tbs rice wine or dry sherry
2 tsps sugar
3 tbs canola oil
1½ lbs skinless and boneless chicken breast, cut into strips (see box, right)
½ lb snow peas, cut in half
1–2 small green chilies, seeded and finely chopped, to taste
2 garlic cloves, minced
2 ripe mangoes, sliced

1 Mix the cornstarch with ⅔ cup water, the soy sauce, rice wine, and sugar. Set aside. Heat the oil in a wok, add the chicken in batches, and stir-fry for 5 minutes.

2 Return all the chicken to the wok, add the snow peas, chilies, and garlic, and stir-fry for 1–2 minutes. Add the soy sauce mixture and stir-fry until thickened.

3 Add the mango slices and stir-fry for 30 seconds. Add more soy sauce if you like, and serve at once.

MALAYSIAN CHICKEN

Serves 4

1 tb cornstarch
2 tbs fish sauce, or more to taste
1½ cups fresh orange juice
1 tsp sugar
3 tbs canola oil
1½ lbs skinless and boneless chicken breast, cut into strips (see box, right)
1 large red bell pepper, cored, seeded, and cut into thin strips
2 garlic cloves, minced
6–8 scallions, thinly sliced
¼ cup chopped fresh coriander (cilantro)

1 Mix the cornstarch with the fish sauce, orange juice, and sugar. Set aside. Heat the oil in a wok, add the chicken in batches, and stir-fry for 2 minutes.

2 Return all the chicken to the wok, add the red bell pepper and garlic, and stir-fry for 5 minutes. Add the orange juice mixture and stir-fry until thickened.

3 Add the scallions and coriander and stir-fry for 30 seconds. Add more fish sauce if you like, and serve at once.

CUTTING CHICKEN FOR STIR-FRIES

Chicken is cut on the diagonal so that it cooks quickly.

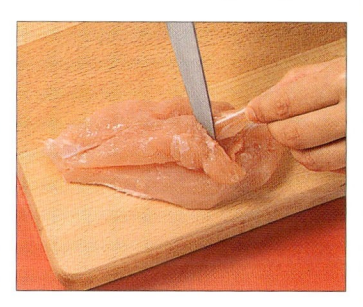

With a small, sharp knife, cut away the white stringy tendon from underneath the breast and detach the fillet.

Cut the chicken breast and fillet on the diagonal into thin strips about ¼-inch wide. To make this easier, you can freeze the chicken for about an hour beforehand.

BONELESS CHICKEN

CHICKEN POT PIE

Crisp, golden pastry conceals a creamy chicken and vegetable filling. Pot pie is always a family favorite – and this quick and easy version is no exception.

Serves 4

2 carrots, sliced	¼–½ tsp dry mustard
2 parsnips, sliced	Salt and freshly ground pepper
2½ cups hot chicken stock	¾ lb skinless and boneless cooked chicken, cubed
2 tbs butter	
1 onion, finely chopped	1 cup heavy cream
2 celery stalks, roughly chopped	½ lb frozen puff pastry, thawed
1 heaping tb all-purpose flour	Beaten egg for glazing
10-oz package frozen fava beans or peas, thawed	

POT PIE

American pot pies originated in Pennsylvania, where they were traditionally made with chicken and vegetables and topped with a layer of homemade flat noodles shaped into discs or squares. Thrifty Pennsylvanian Dutch cooks would simmer a stewing chicken whole with onions, root vegetables, and seasonings, then remove every scrap of meat from the bones and use it to make the pie filling with the thickened stock and fresh vegetables, usually mushrooms. The end result was homey, filling, and very tasty.
The recipe here is a shortcut version using frozen puff pastry, and is every bit as good as the original.

1 Cook the carrots and parsnips in the stock for 5 minutes or until just tender. Drain and reserve the stock. Melt the butter in a clean pan, add the onion and celery, and cook gently for 5 minutes until softened. Sprinkle in the flour and stir for 1 minute.

2 Gradually add the stock and bring to a boil, stirring. Simmer for 2 minutes. Stir in the beans or peas, the mustard, and salt and pepper to taste. Let cool, stir in the root vegetables, chicken, and cream, and turn into a 6-cup baking dish or casserole.

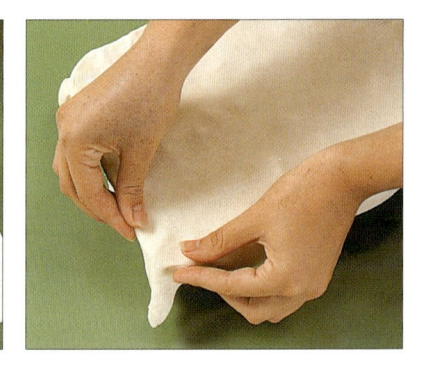

3 Roll out the pastry and cut a lid slightly larger than the dish. Place over the filling and fold under the excess to make a stand-up edge. Crimp the edge, and glaze the top with the beaten egg. Bake in a preheated 400°F oven for 20 minutes.

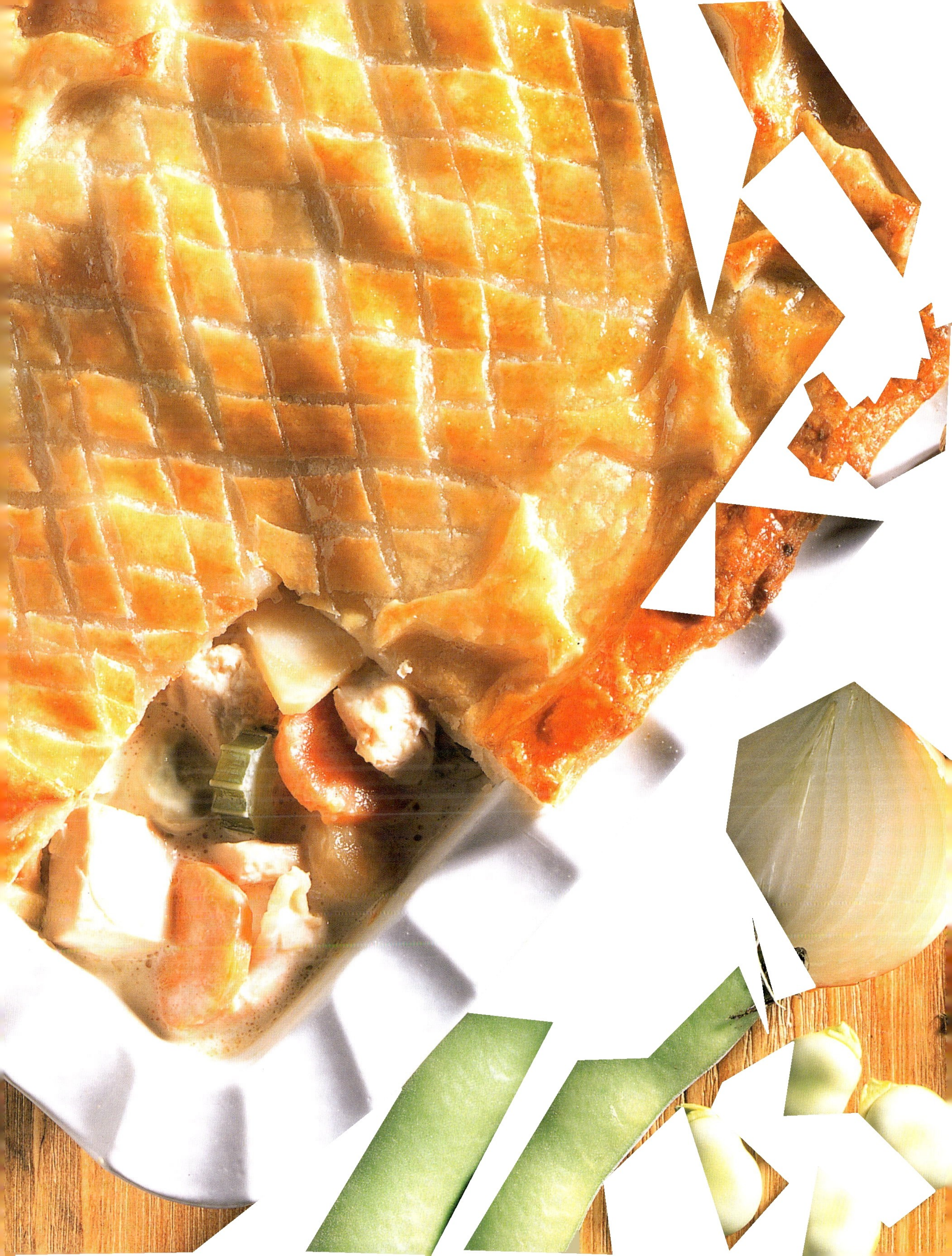

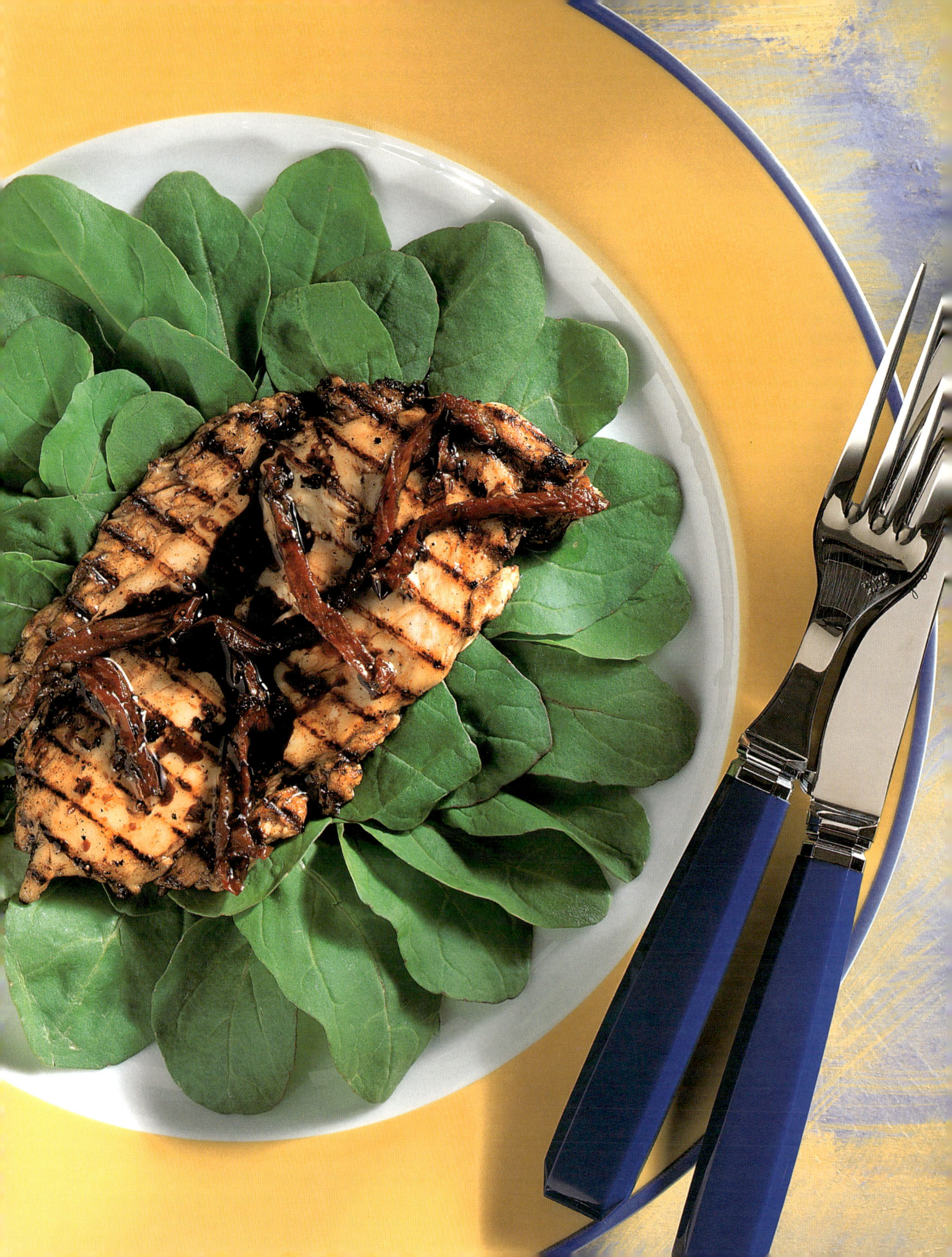

BONELESS CHICKEN

CHICKEN SOL E LUNA

Fresh and light, this simple main course is filled with ripe, gutsy flavor. For a summer meal, it needs no more accompaniment than a loaf of crusty Italian bread and a bottle of chilled dry white wine.

Serves 4

4 large skinless and boneless chicken breast halves	Salt and freshly ground pepper
	2 cups arugula (see box, right)
½ cup virgin olive oil	¼ cup thinly sliced sun-dried tomatoes in olive oil
3 tbs balsamic vinegar	

Finishing touches
Serve with lemon or lime wedges for squeezing.

ARUGULA

This salad green has a strong peppery bite, which is delicious when mixed with other salad greens, or when used as a bed of leaves under fillets of poultry, meat, or fish – as it is with the chicken in this recipe. Originally grown only in Europe, where it is called **rucola** *in Italy, and rocket in England, it is now widely available in most gourmet stores and markets. It is usually sold in bunches with the roots attached. Make sure to wash arugula thoroughly before use, because there is often grit or sand hidden between the leaves. It goes limp quite quickly, so once washed, use it immediately or store it in a plastic bag in the refrigerator until ready to use.*

1 Put the chicken between waxed paper and flatten slightly by beating with a rolling pin. Place in a non-metallic dish. Whisk together the oil and vinegar with pepper to taste and pour over the chicken. Cover and marinate for about 1 hour.

2 Put 2 pieces of chicken on a preheated lightly oiled cast-iron pan and cook over high heat for 3–5 minutes on each side, pressing down firmly with a spatula to keep the meat flat. Repeat with the remaining pieces of chicken.

3 Arrange the arugula on warmed plates, sprinkle with salt and pepper to taste, and place the chicken on top. Add the marinade and tomatoes to the pan and stir until hot, then spoon over the chicken. Serve at once.

BONELESS CHICKEN

SPECIAL CHEF'S SALAD

A traditional chef's salad is made extra-special with Italian ham and cheese, frilly-edged salad leaves, cherry tomatoes, and tiny quail's eggs. The end result is fresh and light – and full of flavor.

Serves 4

¾ lb skinless and boneless cooked chicken, preferably smoked	8 quail's eggs, or 4 hen's eggs, hard-boiled
4 thin slices prosciutto	12 small or cherry tomatoes
½ lb Fontina cheese	Light Thousand Island Dressing (see box, right) for serving
½ head frisée or red leaf lettuce	

Seasonal choice
Use a combination of salad leaves, such as oak leaf or lamb's lettuce, radicchio, and arugula instead of the frisée.

LIGHT THOUSAND ISLAND DRESSING

This popular dressing is made light and fresh by using half plain yogurt and half mayonnaise and adding sun-dried tomatoes for extra flavor. Put ½ cup mayonnaise and ½ cup plain yogurt in a bowl and add ½ finely diced red bell pepper, 2 finely diced scallions, 2 tbs finely chopped sun-dried tomatoes in olive oil, 1 tb bottled chili sauce, and salt and freshly ground pepper to taste. Beat well to mix. Cover and chill for at least 2 hours. Taste for seasoning, stir well, and sprinkle with more chopped sun-dried tomatoes before serving.

1 Cut the chicken, prosciutto, and cheese into thin strips of the same size. Tear the frisée into manageable pieces and arrange the leaves on a large serving platter, with the frilly edges to the outside.

2 Arrange the chicken and cheese slices on top of the frisée, alternating them to make an attractive pattern. Roll up the prosciuttto and place it next to the chicken and cheese.

3 Shell and halve the eggs. Cut the tomatoes into quarters lengthwise. Arrange the eggs and tomatoes around the prosciutto and serve at room temperature, with the dressing.

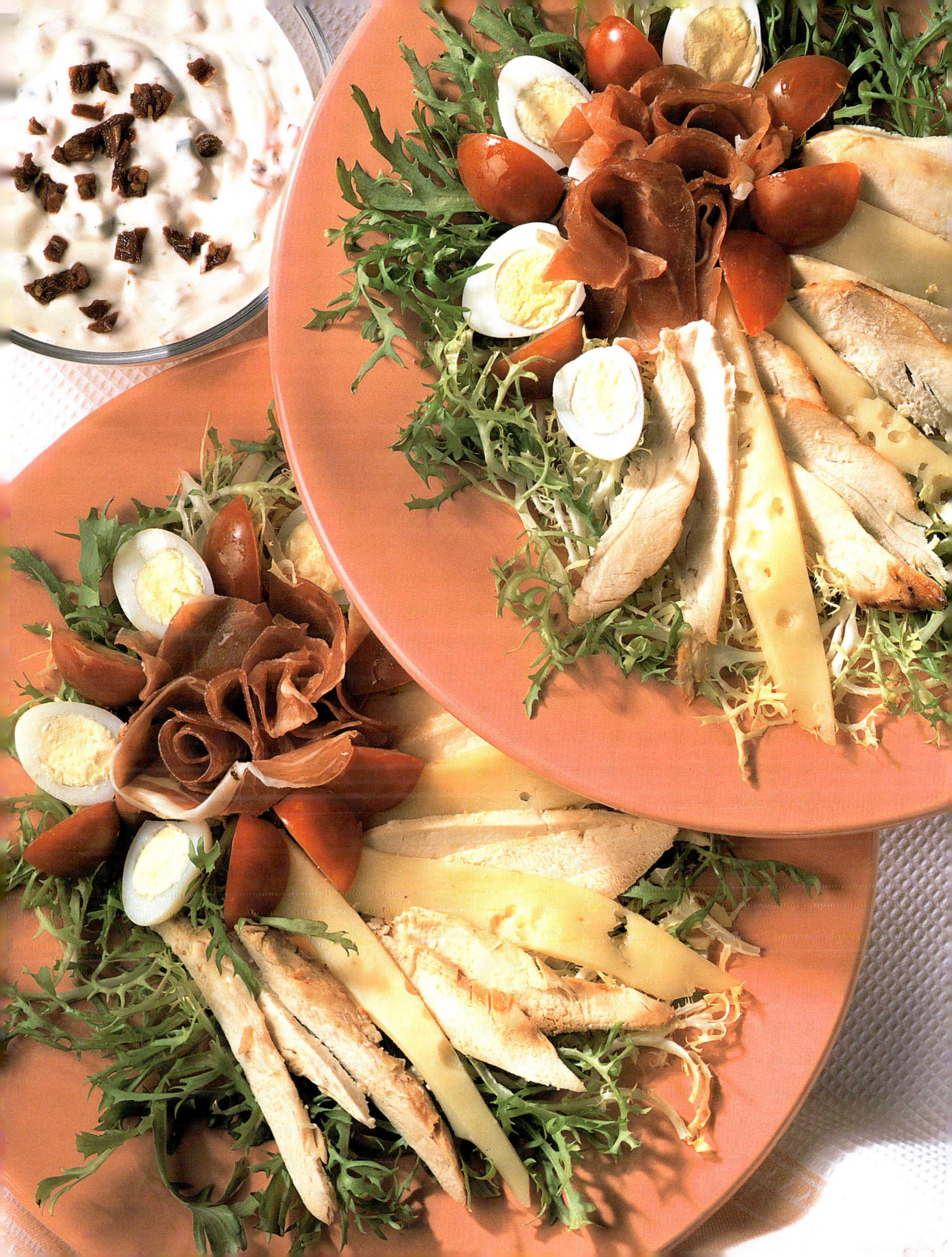

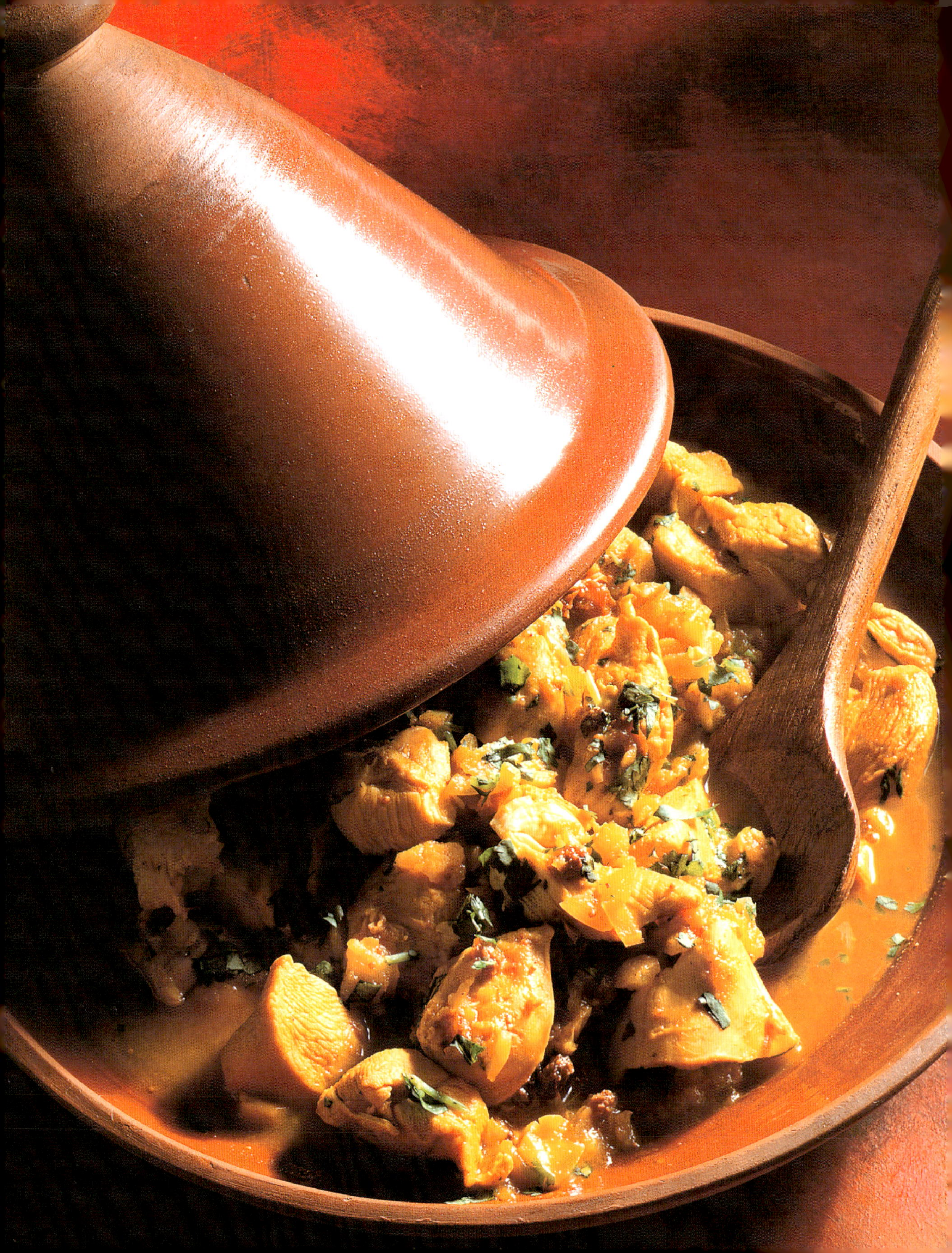

BONELESS CHICKEN

CHICKEN TAGINE

Spicy Moroccan tagine is given a tangy sweet touch with dried fruits and freshly squeezed orange juice. To offset the richness of flavor and color, serve this with bowls of boiled white rice and plain yogurt.

Serves 4

2 tbs canola oil	¼ cup fresh orange juice
1 onion, finely chopped	½ lb package pitted mixed dried fruits, chopped
1 garlic clove, finely chopped	Salt and freshly ground pepper
1 tsp each ground ginger, cumin, and turmeric	1½ lbs skinless and boneless chicken breast meat, cut into large cubes
⅛ tsp ground cinnamon	
1 tb tomato paste	2 tbs chopped fresh coriander (cilantro)
2½ cups chicken stock	

MOROCCAN TAGINE

This dish takes its name from the earthenware pot in which it is traditionally cooked. Looking like a cone-shaped hat, the tagine is designed so that all the natural juices of the food are retained and do not evaporate. You can buy tagines like the one in the photograph from specialty kitchenware shops and ethnic stores, but they are not suitable for cooking on top of the stove and are best kept just for serving as here – or for cooking in the oven. There are many versions of this recipe in Morocco, some with lamb as well as chicken, and some with chickpeas (garbanzos) and vegetables instead of the fruits used here.

1 Heat the oil in a large pan, add the onion, garlic, and ground spices and cook gently for 5 minutes or until fragrant. Stir in the tomato paste and stock, and bring to a boil, stirring.

2 Add the orange juice, dried fruits, and salt and pepper to taste. Cover and simmer gently for 20 minutes or until the fruits have softened and the juices reduced slightly.

3 Add the chicken, cover, and simmer gently, stirring occasionally, for 20 minutes or until tender. Add the chopped coriander, taste for seasoning, and serve hot.

BONELESS CHICKEN

Chicken and Pasta Salad

Nuggets of chicken are tossed with bow-tie pasta, blue cheese, and diced peppers to make a substantial main-dish salad. A nutty vinaigrette with herbs and garlic is the perfect complement.

Serves 4–6

½ lb bow-tie pasta	1 red and 1 yellow or green bell pepper, cored, seeded, and diced
Salt and freshly ground pepper	
¼ lb blue cheese such as Roquefort (see box, right)	½ lb skinless and boneless cooked chicken
⅓ cup hazelnut oil	2–3 tbs chopped fresh parsley
2 tbs white wine vinegar	Salad greens for serving
2 garlic cloves, minced	Pitted black olives for garnish

ROQUEFORT CHEESE

This is a very special cheese, some say the "king of cheeses," from southwest France, where it is ripened for a minimum of 3 months in the limestone caves of Les Causses near the village of Roquefort. It is a blue-veined cheese made from ewe's milk with a creamy texture and piquant, quite salty taste. Look for the red sheep on the wrapper when buying.

1 Cook the pasta in boiling salted water for 10 minutes or until al dente (tender but firm to the bite). Meanwhile, mash half the blue cheese in a large bowl and add the oil, vinegar, garlic, and ground pepper to taste. Whisk this mixture until thickened.

2 Drain the pasta well, add to the dressing while still hot, and toss well to coat. Let cool to room temperature, tossing occasionally. Add the diced bell peppers and toss well until evenly combined with the pasta and dressing.

3 Dice the chicken and the remaining cheese. Gently fold into the salad with the parsley, and taste for seasoning. Transfer the salad to a bowl lined with salad greens and garnish with olives. Serve at room temperature.

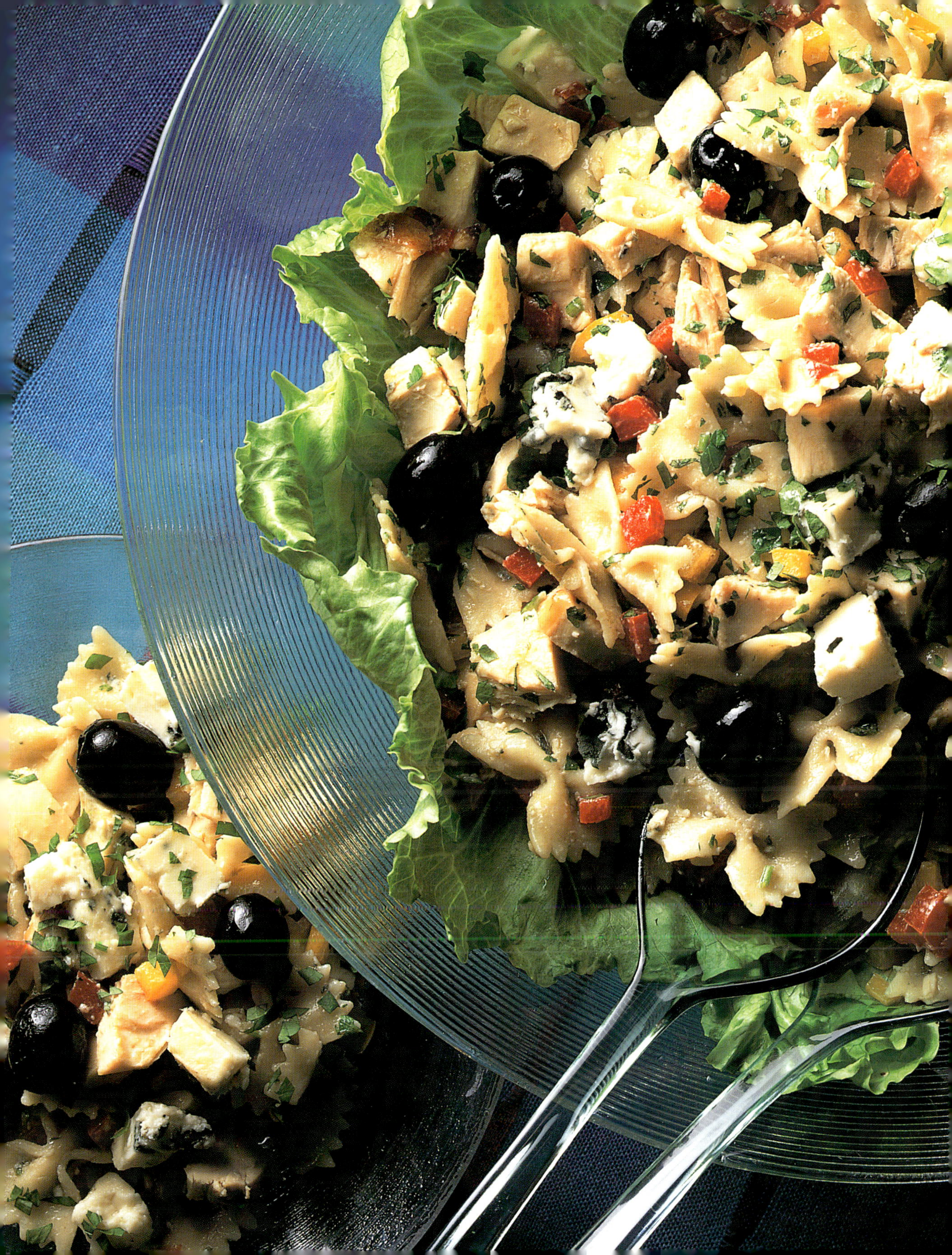

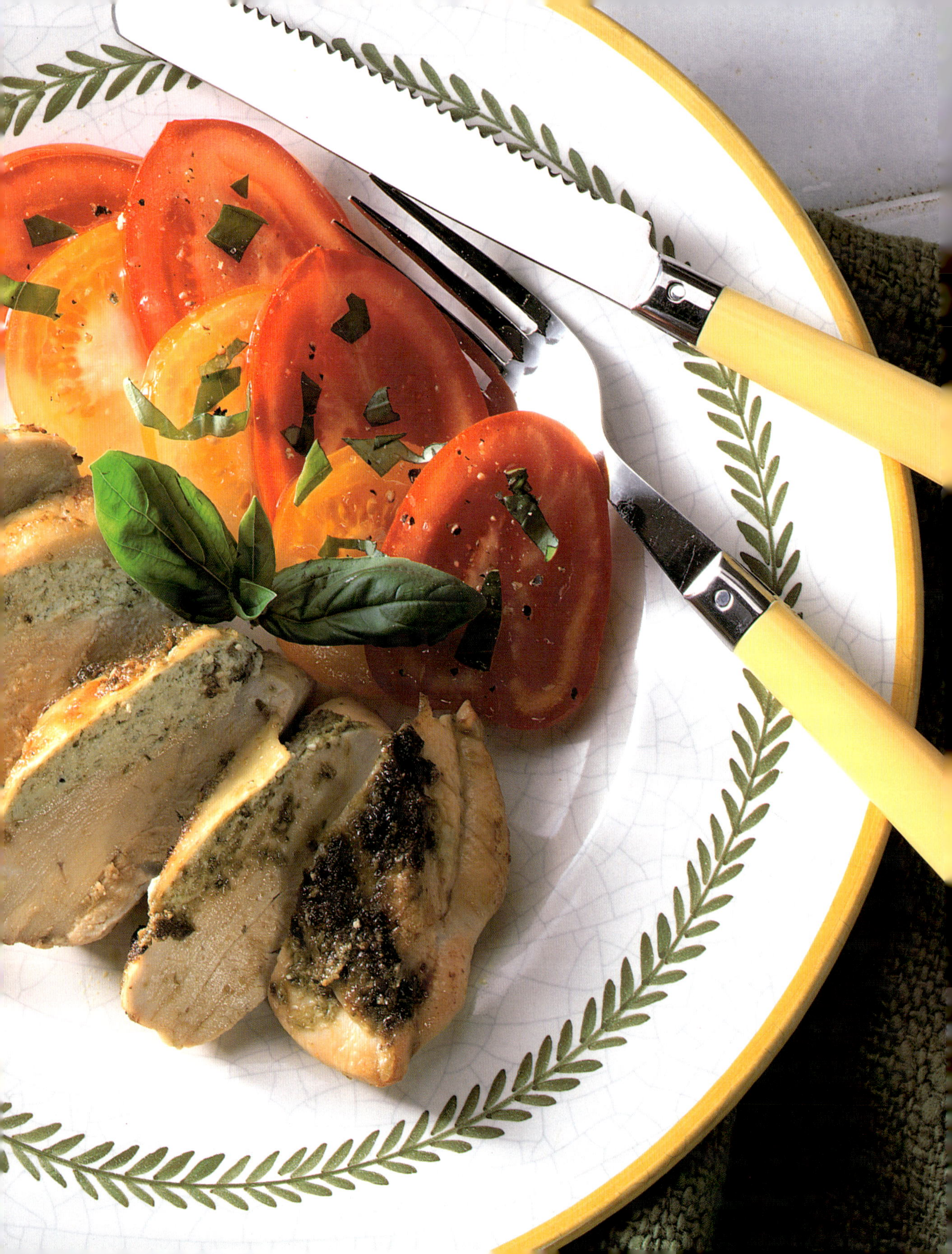

BONELESS CHICKEN

Pesto Chicken

Chicken breast "pockets" are stuffed with ricotta and pesto to make the meat moist, very tender, and packed full of flavor. This clever technique is simple, and only takes a few minutes to prepare.

Serves 4

6 ozs ricotta cheese	2 tsps virgin olive oil
2 tbs pesto (see box, right)	Fresh basil sprigs for garnish
Freshly ground pepper	
4 large boneless chicken breast halves, with skin on	

Special touches
Use minced garlic and chopped fresh herbs instead of the pesto, and cream cheese instead of the ricotta.

> **PESTO**
>
> *A good-quality commercial pesto is fine for the filling in this recipe. The kind sold fresh in Italian markets is best if you can get it, but if you have time, you can make pesto yourself – it freezes very well for up to a month, so it's worth making a big batch. Put 2 cups loosely packed fresh basil leaves, 2 peeled and halved garlic cloves, ¼ cup pine nuts, and ½ cup extra-virgin olive oil in a blender or food processor and work to a smooth purée. Spoon into a bowl, add ½ cup freshly grated Parmesan cheese and 2 tbs freshly grated pecorino cheese, and beat well to mix. Taste and add salt and pepper if necessary.*

1 Put the ricotta in a bowl with 2 tsps of the pesto and pepper to taste. Beat well to mix. Carefully lift up the skin of each chicken breast half and ease it away from the flesh with your fingers to make a pocket.

2 Spoon the cheese mixture into the pockets and smooth the skin over it with your hands so that the chicken retains its shape. Put the chicken in a single layer in a lightly oiled baking dish.

3 Spread the chicken with the remaining pesto, drizzle with oil, and sprinkle with pepper. Bake in a preheated 400°F oven for 20 minutes or until tender. Cut into slices on the diagonal and serve hot, garnished with basil.

BONELESS CHICKEN

THAI CHICKEN

Perfumed with lemon grass, ginger, coriander, coconut, and lime, this quick and easy stir-fry evokes the fragrant flavors of the East. Red hot chilies add a powerful spicy kick, to which homemade coconut rice is the perfect foil.

Serves 4

2 large garlic cloves, roughly chopped	2 tsps turmeric
2-inch piece fresh ginger root, peeled and roughly chopped	2 14-oz cans coconut milk
	2 lbs skinless and boneless chicken thighs, cut into bite-size pieces
2 small fresh red or green chilies, seeded and roughly chopped	Juice of 1 lime
1 stalk lemon grass, lower part only, sliced	3 tbs Thai fish sauce
	Coconut rice (see box, right) for serving
6 sprigs fresh coriander (cilantro), stems and leaves separated	

COCONUT RICE

This traditional Thai dish is simply rice that is cooked in a mixture of coconut milk and water rather than water alone. The texture is soft and creamy and the flavor subtle. Put 2¼ cups canned coconut milk in a pan, add 1½ cups water, 1 bruised stalk lemon grass, and ½ tsp salt. Bring to a boil, add 1½ cups long-grain rice, and stir once. Half cover with a lid and simmer over gentle heat for 20 minutes. Remove from the heat, cover the pan tightly, and let the rice stand for at least 5 minutes or until ready to serve. Discard the lemon grass before serving, taste, and add more salt if you like.

1 Put the garlic, ginger, chilies, lemon grass, and coriander stems in a food processor. Add the turmeric and a few spoonfuls of thick cream from the top of the coconut milk, and work the mixture to a paste.

2 Put the spice paste in a wok, add the remaining coconut cream and milk, and bring to a boil, stirring. Simmer, stirring, until the coconut milk reduces and thickens slightly.

3 Add the chicken, lime juice, and fish sauce. Cook, stirring frequently, for 40 minutes or until the chicken is tender. Sprinkle with the coriander leaves and serve hot, with coconut rice.

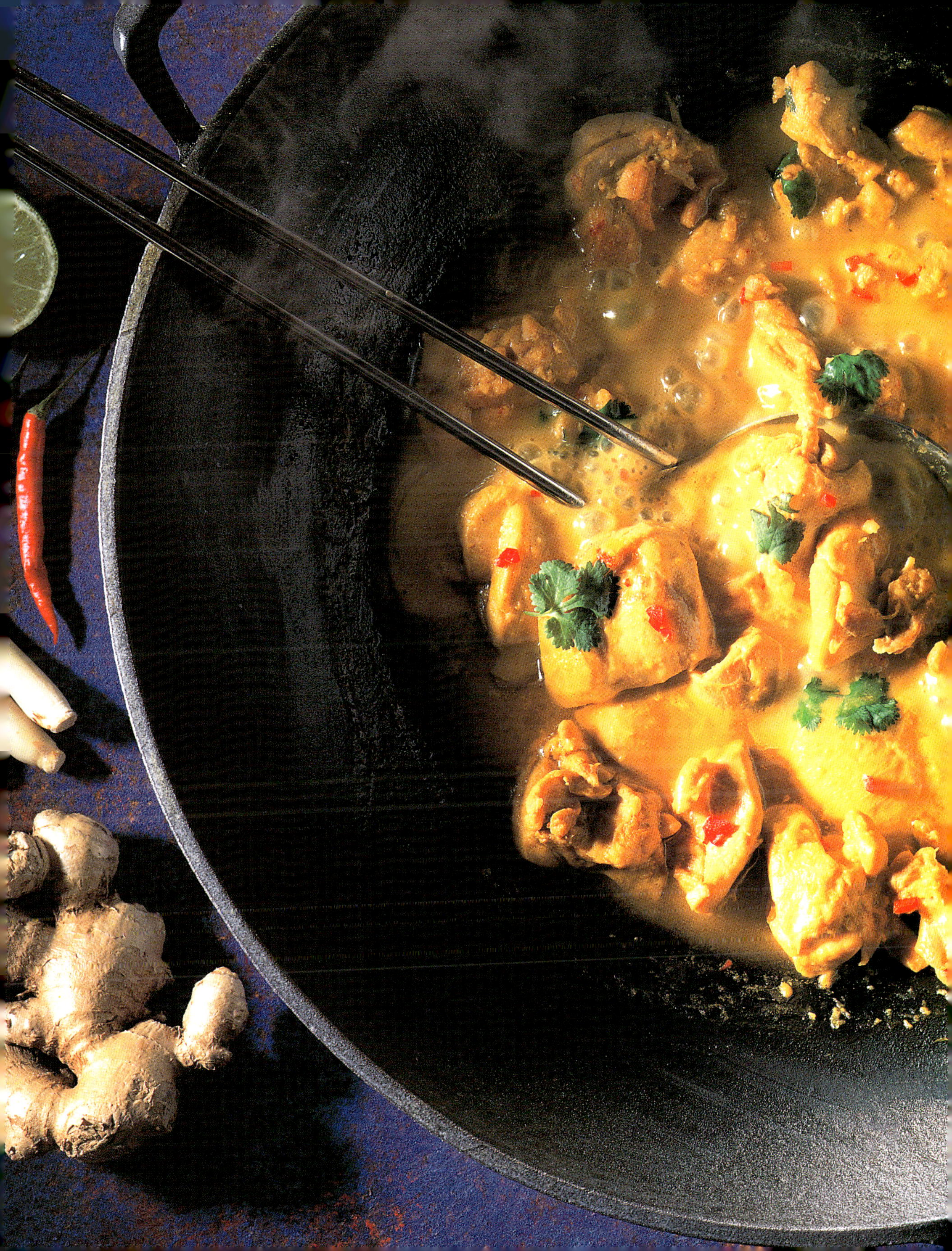

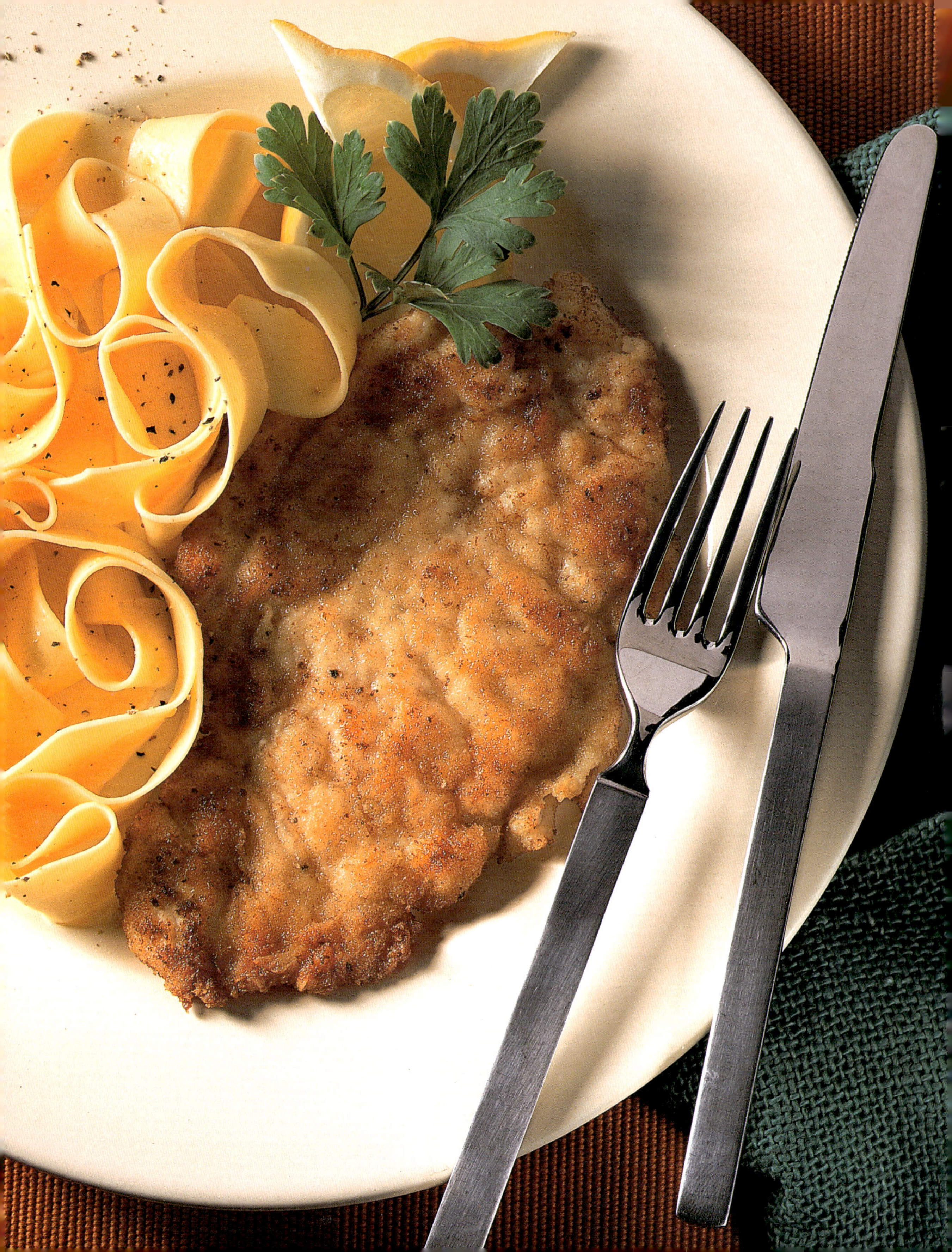

BONELESS CHICKEN

Chicken Schnitzels

Chicken scaloppine are shallow-fried in a crisp and crunchy coating. Here they are served with wide egg noodles for a substantial meal.

Serves 4

4 skinless and boneless chicken breast halves	About ½ cup fine dry breadcrumbs
Salt and freshly ground pepper	About 6 tbs canola oil
3 tbs all-purpose flour	Lemon wedges and parsley sprigs for serving
1 egg, beaten	

Seasonal choice
This dish can be served with a crisp green salad instead of the noodles.

SCHNITZEL

This is the German word for cutlet, used to describe any meat, poultry, or fish that is pounded very thin, then coated in seasoned flour, beaten egg, and fine breadcrumbs. The most famous schnitzel of all is the Austrian **Wienerschnitzel,** *a specialty of the capital, Vienna. Schnitzels are traditionally shallow-fried in hot oil until crisp and golden, then served at once with a garnish of lemon and parsley. The secret of their crispness is leaving the schnitzels uncovered when chilling them in the refrigerator before frying. This hardens the crumb coating so that when the schnitzels are placed in very hot oil they become crisp and golden.*

1 Put the chicken breasts and fillets between 2 sheets of waxed paper and pound them with a rolling pin until they are flattened. Season each piece of chicken with salt and pepper.

2 Coat the chicken first in the flour, then in the beaten egg, and then finally in the breadcrumbs. Chill, uncovered, for at least 30 minutes. Heat 3 tbs oil in a non-stick skillet until hot.

3 Add 2 schnitzels and fry over high heat for 3 minutes on each side. Drain on paper towels. Wipe the pan clean and repeat with more oil and schnitzels. Serve hot, with lemon wedges and parsley sprigs.

BONELESS CHICKEN

MEE GORENG

In this simple version of the famous Thai specialty, chicken, shrimp, and noodles are stir-fried together to make an absolute feast of flavors and colors.

Serves 4

½ lb dried egg noodles (see box, right)	½–¾ lb raw shrimp, peeled and chopped
Salt	2 tbs Thai fish sauce, plus more for serving
3 tbs canola oil	
1 small onion, finely chopped	1 cup chicken stock or water
1 garlic clove, finely chopped	1–2 tbs sesame oil
1 red chili, finely chopped	
1 lb skinless and boneless cooked chicken, cut into small dice	

Special touches
Rice can be used instead of noodles to make Indonesian *Nasi Goreng*.

ASIAN NOODLES

Mee *is the Thai for noodles, of which there are many different kinds. In Thailand, Mee Goreng is made with a type of fresh rice noodle, or vermicelli, called* **lai fan**. *These noodles are pure white in color, flat, and wide, and they need to be soaked and boiled in water, then rinsed thoroughly before use. The Thais often stir-fry them, or deep-fry them until crisp in very hot oil to make another famous dish –* **Mee Krob**. *For this simple version of Mee Goreng, use dried Chinese egg noodles, available from any supermarket. Choose either fine thread egg noodles or medium egg noodles, whichever you prefer.*

1 Fill a large pan with salted water. Bring the water to a boil; break-up and add the noodles. Cook for 4 minutes or according to package directions.

2 Heat the oil in a wok, add the onion, garlic, and chili, and stir-fry for 1–2 minutes. Add the chicken, shrimp, and fish sauce and toss over high heat for about 2 minutes until the shrimp are pink.

3 Drain the noodles, add to the wok with the stock, and toss well to mix. Turn into a warmed bowl and sprinkle with sesame oil. Serve at once, with fish sauce passed separately.

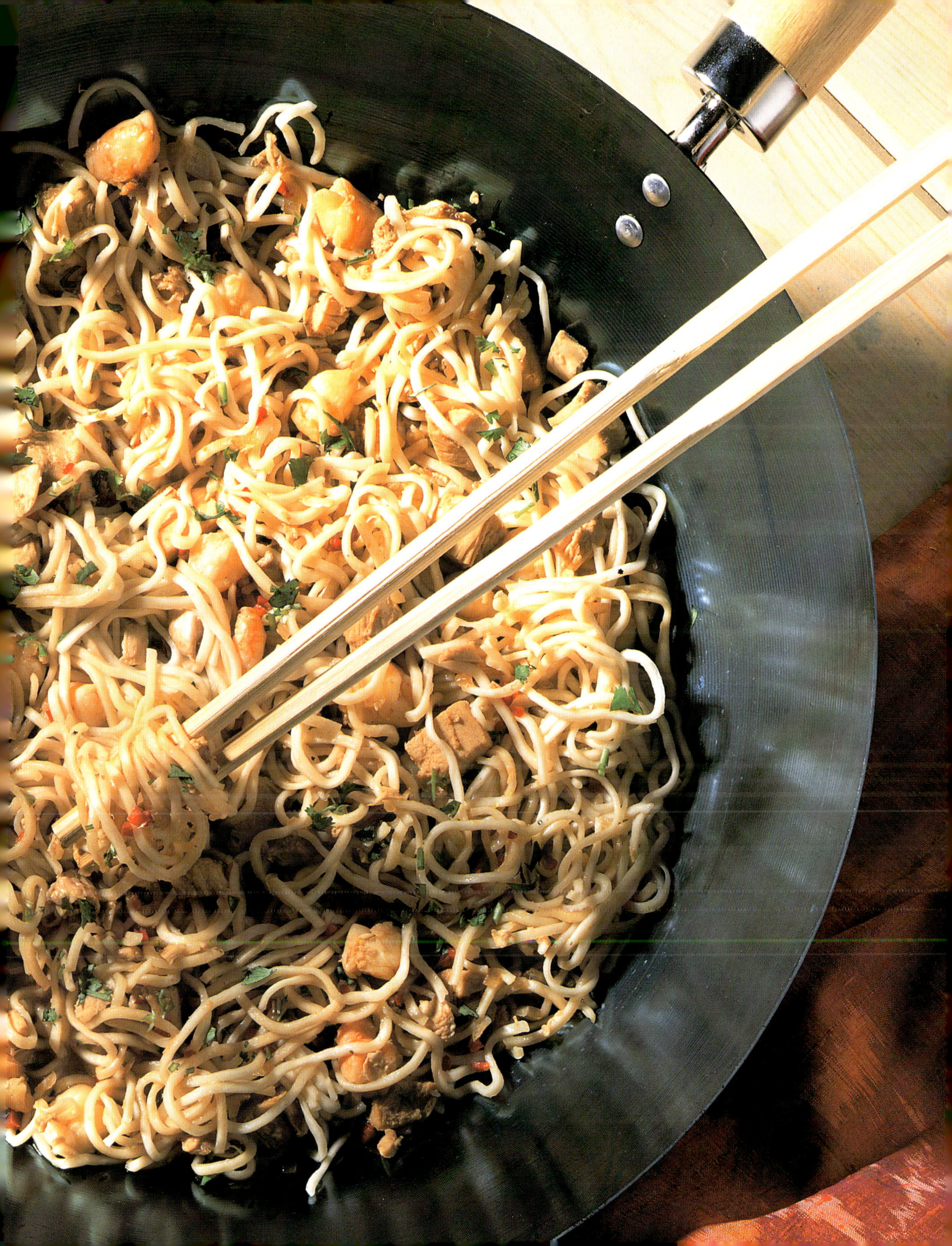

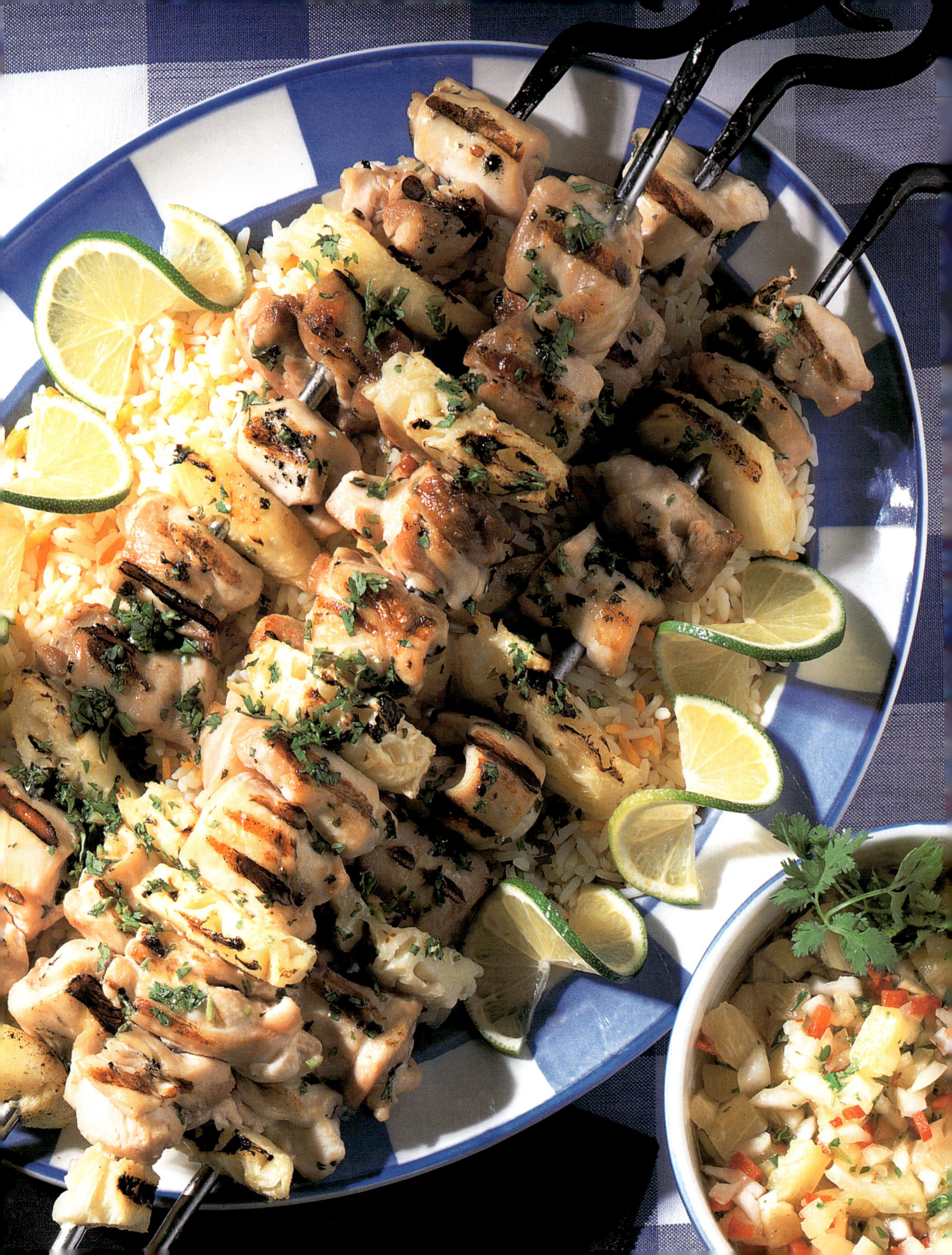

BONELESS CHICKEN

CHICKEN AND PINEAPPLE KEBABS

Skewers of juicy chicken and sweet ripe pineapple both look and taste good on a bed of coconut rice (page 88). Fruit salsa is the perfect accompaniment.

Serves 4

8 skinless and boneless chicken thighs, cut into 1-inch pieces	Juice of 1 lime
	2 garlic cloves, minced
1 small pineapple, peeled, cored, and cut into chunks with juice reserved	Lime twists and chopped fresh coriander (cilantro) for garnish
1 cup canned coconut milk	Fruit Salsa (see box, right) for serving
2 tbs virgin olive oil	
¼ cup chopped fresh coriander (cilantro)	

> ### FRUIT SALSA
> *Cool, refreshing salsas go well with hot grilled poultry and meat, and sweet and juicy pineapple mixed with tangy onion and bell pepper is especially good with chicken. Peel, core, and finely chop 1 small fresh pineapple, and place in a bowl with its juice. Finely chop 1 small red bell pepper, discarding the core and seeds, 1 small onion, and a few fresh coriander (cilantro) sprigs. Add to the chopped pineapple in the bowl with 3 tbs extra-virgin olive oil, 2 tbs fresh lime juice, and salt and freshly ground pepper to taste. Stir well to mix, cover, and chill in the refrigerator for at least 1 hour before serving.*

1 Mix the chicken with the pineapple juice and all the remaining ingredients except the pineapple chunks, garnish, and salsa. Cover and marinate in the refrigerator for at least 1 hour.

2 Thread the chicken pieces onto oiled metal kebab skewers, alternating them with pieces of pineapple. Reserve the marinade in the bowl.

3 Grill the chicken for about 15 minutes, turning it often and brushing it with the marinade from the bowl. Serve hot, garnished with lime twists and coriander. Pass the salsa separately.

Recipe Index

Andalusian chicken 39
Apple-glazed Cornish hens 11
Asian stir-fries 75

Baby chickens with pancetta 23
Bang bang chicken 43
Bell peppers, roasted 44
Bouquet garni 8
Breadcrumbs, dried 47

Celebration roast chicken 12
Chef's salad, special 80
Chicken
    with forty garlic cloves 20
    Marengo 51
    with mascarpone 59
    en papillote 64
    paprikash 40
    pasanda 60
    and pasta salad 84
    and pineapple kebabs 95
    pinwheels 56
    pot pie 76
    with red wine and grapes 35
    saté 55
    schnitzels 91
    Siam 60
    sol e luna 79
    soup Creole 27
    tagine 83
Chinese chicken 75
Coconut rice 88
Cornish hens
    apple-glazed 11
    with shallots and lemon 17
Creole, chicken soup 27
Crispy chicken 47
Croûtes 20
Curries, simple chicken 60
Cutting chicken for stir-fries 75

Deviled drumsticks 36
Dressing, light Thousand Island 80
Dried breadcrumbs 47
Drumsticks, deviled 36

En papillote, chicken 64

Farmhouse chicken in a pot 8
French roast chicken 19
Fried polenta 59
Frikadeller 67
Fruit salsa 95

Garlic cloves, chicken with forty 20
Grapes, chicken with red wine and 35
Grilled chicken with hot chili salsa 31
Grilled chicken, marinated 36
Grilling whole birds 24

Honey-mustard chicken 36

Jerk chicken 24

Kashmiri chicken 60
Kebabs, chicken and pineapple 95

Light Thousand Island dressing 80

Malaysian chicken 75
Marengo, chicken 51
Marinated grilled chicken 36
Mascarpone, chicken with 59
Meatballs, see Frikadeller
Mee Goreng 92
Moroccan tagine 83

Orange-soy chicken 15

Pancetta
    baby chickens with 23
    and cheese pinwheels 56
Paprikash, chicken 40
Pasanda, chicken 60
Pasta salad, chicken and 84
Peanut sauce 55
Peppers, roasted bell 44
Peppery chicken 44
Pesto chicken 87
Pie, chicken pot 76
Pineapple kebabs, chicken and 95
Pinwheels
    chicken 56
    pancetta and cheese 56
    spinach and ricotta 56
Polenta, fried 59
Pot pie, chicken 76

Red wine and grapes, chicken with 35
Rice
    coconut 88
    Spanish chicken and 48
Roast(ed)
    bell peppers 44
    chicken, celebration 12
    chicken, French 19
    chicken and vegetables 52
    shallots 19

Salad
    chicken and pasta 84
    special chef's 80
    warm chicken 68
Salsa, fruit 95
Saltimbocca 71
Sandwich, sautéed chicken, with bacon 72
Saté, chicken 55
Sauce, peanut 55
Sautéed chicken sandwich with bacon 72
Schnitzels, chicken 91
Shaker chicken 28
Shallots
    and lemon, Cornish hens with 17
    roasted 19
Siam, chicken 60
Simple chicken curries 60
Soup Creole, chicken 27
Spanish chicken and rice 48
Special chef's salad 80
Spinach and ricotta pinwheels 56
Stir-fries, Asian 75
Stock, chicken 6
Stuffing, lemon-herb 12

Tagine, chicken 83
Tandoori chicken 36
Tarragon cream chicken 32
Teriyaki chicken 63
Thai chicken 88
Thousand Island dressing, light 80

Vegetables, roasted chicken and 52

Warm chicken salad 68

Acknowledgments

Photographer's assistant Sid Sideris
Food preparation Maddalena Bastianelli
Production consultant Lorraine Baird
Index Madeline Weston
Illustrations Stanley Sweet